ELIZABETH
DAVID

I'LL BE WITH YOU
IN THE SQUEEZING
OF A LEMON

PENGUIN BOOKS

PENGUIN BOOKS

Published by the Penguin Group. Penguin Books Ltd, 27 Wrights Lane,
London w8 5tz, England. Penguin Books USA Inc., 375 Hudson Street,
New York, New York 10014, USA. Penguin Books Australia Ltd, Ringwood,
Victoria, Australia. Penguin Books Canada Ltd, 10 Alcorn Avenue, Toronto,
Ontario, Canada m4v 3b2. Penguin Books (NZ) Ltd, 182–190 Wairau Road,
Auckland 10, New Zealand · Penguin Books Ltd, Registered Offices: Har-
mondsworth, Middlesex, England · **These extracts are taken from** *French
Provincial Cooking, An Omelette and a Glass of Wine, Summer Cooking, A
Book of Mediterranean Food, Spices, Salts and Aromatics in the English
Kitchen, French Country Cooking* **and** *English Bread and Yeast Cookery,* **all
published by Penguin Books.** This edition published 1995 · Copyright ©
Elizabeth David, 1960, 1962, 1965, 1966, 1970, 1977, 1984, 1987, 1988. This
selection copyright © the Estate of Elizabeth David, 1995 · The moral right of the
author has been asserted · All rights reserved · Typeset by Datix International
Limited, Bungay, Suffolk. Printed in England by Clays Ltd, St Ives plc · Except in
the United States of America, this book is sold subject to the condition that it shall
not, by way of trade or otherwise, be lent, re-sold, hired out, or otherwise
circulated without the publisher's prior consent in any form of binding or
cover other than that in which it is published and without a similar condition
including this condition being imposed on the subsequent purchaser ·
10 9 8 7 6 5 4 3 2 1

CONTENTS

Paris and Normandy 1

The True Emulsion 13

Picnics 21

Juanita's Tortilla 28

Golden Delicious 30

Italian Dishes in Foreign Kitchens 35

Chez Barattero 45

Measurements and Temperatures 62

Les Potages: Soups 66

Cassoulet Toulousain 76

'I'll be with You in the Squeezing of a Lemon' 79

Cottage Loaves 85

Paris and Normandy

from *French Provincial Cooking*

Although I did not realize it at the time, it was by way of Norman cookery that I first learned to appreciate French food. Torn, most willingly, from an English boarding school at the age of sixteen, to live with a middle-class French family in Passy, it was only some time later that I tumbled to the fact that even for a Parisian family who owned a small farm in Normandy, the Robertots were both exceptionally greedy and exceptionally well fed. Their cook, a young woman called Léontine, was bullied from morning till night, and how she had the spirit left to produce such delicious dishes I cannot now imagine. Twice a week at dawn Madame, whose purple face was crowned with a magnificent mass of white hair, went off to do the marketing at Les Halles, the central markets, where she bought all the provisions, including flowers for the flat. I don't think any shopping at all was done locally, except for things like milk and bread. She would return at about ten o'clock, two bursting black shopping bags in each hand, puffing, panting, mopping her brow, and looking as if she was about to have a stroke. Indeed, poor Madame, after I had been in Paris about a year, her doctor told her that high blood pressure made it imperative for her to diet. Her diet consisted of cutting out meat once a week. With Friday a fish day anyway, this actually meant two days without meat. On Wednesdays, the day chosen, Madame would sit at table, the tears welling up in her eyes as she watched us helping ourselves to our *rôti de veau* or *boeuf à la cuillère*. It was soon given up, that diet. Her grown-up children, two of whom were afflicted with a tragic eye disease and were probably going blind, simply could not bear to watch her sufferings – although, of course, they were not prepared to go so far as to share in her privations. Denise, the only able-bodied daughter, was the greediest girl I had ever seen. She worked as secretary to a world-famous Parisian surgeon, and came home every day to the midday meal. Before she took off her hat and coat she would shout out to Léontine to know what was for lunch. Munching through two helpings of everything she would entertain us to gruesome details of the operations performed by her employer.

It never occurred to me at the time to wonder whether she had really witnessed these harrowing sights or if it was just her own way of expressing her family's morbid preoccupation with death and disaster, which reached its peak every Thursday. For Thursday was Madame's *jour*, and not even the really remarkable turn-out of cakes and *petits fours*, mostly made by Léontine, reconciled us to the fact that courtesy demanded we put in an appearance and listen to stories of the appalling catastrophes which had befallen during the week la cousine Anne-Marie, Tante Berthe, her daughter Marguerite, mortally stricken with diabetes, and about half a dozen other ladies always dressed from head to foot in deepest black.

To make up for the ordeal of Thursday afternoon, the boarders (there were only three of us) soon got round to finding some pretext for not being present at Friday lunch. Ever since those days it has remained a mystery to me how people who were so fond of good food and who knew so much about it could endure to eat the boiled salt cod which was the regular Friday lunch. Grey, slimy, in great hideous flakes, it lay plonked on the dish without benefit of sauce or garnish of any kind. At that time I had not even heard of Provençal cooking, or of any of the excellent ways they prepare salt cod in the south, and did not of course know how the people of Provence would scoff at the very idea of a Norman cook producing a decent dish of *morue*. In any case, to avoid this horror, we used to treat ourselves to lunch in a students' restaurant near the Sorbonne, where we thought ourselves lucky to eat egg mayonnaise and a dish of *petits pois* without being questioned by the family as to what the morning's lectures had been about.

Another place where we enjoyed ourselves hugely was at the automatic restaurant, in the Boulevard St Michel I think, all shining chromium and terribly noisy, where we got a plate of ham and an orange out of a slot machine for

3

a few francs. Eating here was forbidden by Madame, who considered that neither the *ambiance* nor the food were suitable for young girls. We used to memorize the menu posted up outside some approved restaurant so that we should have an answer ready when she questioned us. We seldom got away with it, of course, because we were never able to describe the food in the detail required. What appalling *ordures* had been in the so-called *vol-au-vent*? Were the *boulettes de viande* made from beef or veal or lamb? Ah, tiens, *des épinards à la crème*, and did they really contain cream or some horrible *sauce blanche*? Vous ne le savez pas? Mais comment, chère Elisabeth, you did not notice? No, chère Elisabeth had not noticed and did not care, for the fact was that although we enjoyed the good food in the Rue Eugène Delacroix, we were bored with the family's perpetual preoccupation with it, and there was little else to talk to them about; for when they were not actually eating or going to market, Madame and her eldest daughter were either wearing themselves out with long vigils in church or knitting for the poor. We felt stifled by the atmosphere of doom which seemed always imminent in the household, and spent more and more time in our rooms mugging up for our exams and thinking of every possible excuse for not coming in to meals.

So it was only later, after I had come home to England, that I realized in what way the family had fulfilled their task of instilling French culture into at least one of their

British charges. Forgotten were the Sorbonne professors and the yards of Racine learnt by heart, the ground plans of cathedrals I had never seen, and the saga of Napoleon's last days on St Helena. What had stuck was the taste for a kind of food quite ideally unlike anything I had known before. Ever since, I have been trying to catch up with those lost days when perhaps I should have been more profitably employed watching Léontine in her kitchen rather than trudging conscientiously round every museum and picture gallery in Paris.

I do not think that the Robertots spent, as the French are always said to do, a disproportionate amount of their income on food. What with the bargains from Les Halles, the wine arriving in casks from Bordeaux, and cream and butter from their Norman property, their food was lovely without being rich or grand. Above all, as I see it now, it was consistent, all of a piece, and this of course was due to Madame's careful buying. There was none of that jerky feeling you get when the marketing is erratic or careless. So what emerges from those days is not the memory of elaborate sauces or sensational puddings, but rather of beautifully prepared vegetables like *salsifis à la crème*, purées of sorrel, and *pommes mousseline*. Many egg dishes, and soups delicately coloured like summer dresses, coral, ivory or pale green, a salad of rice and tomatoes, another of cold beef, and especially, of course, Léontine's chocolate 5 and apricot soufflés. On soufflé days Denise would suddenly find she was in a fearful hurry to get back to work. This meant that the soufflé was handed to her first. She not only saw to it that she got it before it had had a chance to sink, but if there was enough for a second helping she had first go at that too.

Sometimes I spent part of the Easter or summer holidays with the family at their little Norman farmhouse near Caen. Here a local girl, Marie, took over the cooking, while Léontine returned to her family in the country for what must have been a well-earned rest. The only vivid memory I have of the food in this peaceful and pretty house with its old-fashioned kitchen garden is of tasting mussels for the first time. They were served in a thick creamy sauce which no doubt had cider or white wine in its composition; this seemed to me a most mysterious and extraordinary dish, something which must be quite special to the family or perhaps thought up by Marie, the little village girl, so that when a year or two later I found *moules à la crème* on the menu at Walterspiel's in Munich, at that time one of the most famous restaurants in Europe, I was quite astonished and wondered how it had found its way from that obscure little Norman village all the way to Bavaria. To this day a dish of mussels is one of the first things I ask for upon landing in Northern France, and the

last thing I eat before crossing the Channel to return to

England, for although since that first time I have eaten mussels served in dozens of different ways in many parts of Europe and have cooked them myself hundreds of times, they never seem to have quite the *cachet*, the particular savour, of those mussels of Normandy, so small and sweet in their shining little shells.

To the traveller as yet unacquainted with Norman cookery an impression that perhaps the inhabitants live on duck pâté and *tripes à la mode de Caen* might arouse a faint feeling of apprehension as he walks round a big Norman town such as Rouen. Every two yards there seems to be a *charcuterie*, its windows fairly bursting with all the terrines and galantines, the pâtés and *ballotines*, all made of duck; and the butchers as well as the *charcutiers* display earthenware bowls of ready-cooked tripe, very inviting-looking in its savoury bronze jelly. But neither duck nor tripe, he feels, is quite the dish for every day. There is no need to worry. Take a look round the market in the morning and the spectacle is thoroughly reassuring. The fish is particularly beautiful in its pale, translucent northern way. Delicate rose pink langoustines lie next to miniature scallops in their red-brown shells; great fierce skate and sleek soles are flanked by striped iridescent mackerel, pearly little smelts, and baskets of very small, very black mussels. Here and there an angry-looking red gurnet waits for a customer near a mass of sprawling crabs and a heap of little grey shrimps. Everywhere there is ice and seaweed and a fresh sea smell.

Outside, the vegetable stalls are piled high with Breton artichokes, perfectly round with tightly closed leaves; long, clean, shining leeks; and fluffy green-white cauliflowers. At the next stall an old country woman is displaying carefully bunched salad herbs, chives, chervil, sorrel, radishes and lettuces. So far, it could well be the central market of any one of a score of French towns. But when you get to the dairy stalls, then you know you could only be in the astonishingly productive province of Normandy, where you buy the butter of Isigny and of Gournay carved off a great block, where bowls of thick white cream and the cheeses of Camembert, Livarot, Neufchâtel, Pont l'Evêque, Rouy, Isigny and a dozen other districts ooze with all the richness of the Norman pastures.

How deeply our own roots are in Normandy quickly becomes apparent to the English traveller. The churches, the old timbered houses, the quiet villages, the fruit orchards, the willows hanging over the streams, are familiar. But not the cooking (although I have heard tell of two country dishes which, in effect, must be almost identical with our own rice pudding and apple dumplings, but have never come across them). It is indeed curious that, with such similar pasture lands, we should never have taken to the manufacture of anything like the soft 8 rich cheeses of the Normans, while they have apparently never attemped to make anything in the manner of Cheddar or Gloucester. And while we on the whole prefer to eat our butter with bread and our cream with fruit, the use of these two ingredients in Norman cooking is almost excessively lavish, both of them appearing to possess qualities which make them turn to the consistency of a sauce with very little effort on the part of the cook. When you get melted butter with a trout in Normandy it is difficult to believe that it is not cream. When a chicken or vegetables are served with a cream sauce it is most likely pure cream, unthickened with egg-yolks or flour, although it may well be enriched with Calvados, the cider brandy of Normandy. The quality of this famous Calvados varies enormously (the most reputed comes from the Vallée d'Auge, one of the chief cider districts) and it is rare to come across a really fine old Calvados except in private houses; perhaps in any case it is an acquired taste. In cooking, however, even a comparatively immature Calvados gives to sauces a characteristic flavour which cannot be imitated with any other brandy or spirit, and which I find very delicious, especially with pork and veal. Cider is of course also used in Norman cookery, although not perhaps to the extent generally supposed, and rarely in restaurants, where chefs consider that white wine gives a more delicate flavour and a better colour to the more sophisticated dishes of Norman cookery.

For the rest, the meat in Normandy is of high quality.

The sheep from the salt marshes of the Cotentin yield delicious mutton and lamb; the veal is tender, the beef well nourished; the favourite local pork dishes include the *Andouille de Vire*, a lightly smoked chitterling sausage with a black skin, which is a great deal nicer than it looks, and *rillettes*, that soft, melting kind of potted pork which is to be seen in great pyramids in the *charcuteries*, and which, with the duck pâté and the *andouille*, are the mainstays of a Norman hors-d'œuvre.

Then there are the famous duck dishes made with the *Caneton Rouennais*, which is a very different bird from that of Aylesbury. A cross between a domestic and a wild duck, the breed of Rouen has a flavour, rich and gamey, all its own, due not only to breeding but to the fact that in order to retain their blood they are strangled in a manner which would not be tolerated in this country, where we treat our animals with more consideration than we do our fellow men. Mostly, Rouen ducks are partly roasted, the breast meat carved, and the carcase pressed to extract the blood, which forms an important element in the finished sauce. At Duclair, famous for a breed of duck which is a variation of that of Rouen, the Hôtel de la Poste has no fewer than fourteen ways of presenting duck, including a plain spit-roasted one as well as a very rich *canard au sang* and a *pâté de canard au porto* served in the rugged terrine in which it has cooked. It is interesting to compare these Norman duck pâtés with those of Périgord and Alsace, for they have a quite distinct and different flavour.

As for the renowned *tripes à la mode de Caen*, cooked for about twelve hours with ox feet, cider, Calvados, carrots, onions and herbs, I must confess that nowadays I quail from eating it, let alone from undertaking the cooking of such a dish. It is only at its best when prepared in copious quantities and preferably in a special earthenware pot rather the shape of a flattened-out tea pot, the small opening of which ensures the minimum of evaporation. Formerly, the pot of tripe was carried to the bakery to be cooked in the oven after the bread had been taken out, and nowadays it is more often ordered in a restaurant or bought ready cooked from the butcher or *charcutier* and heated up at home. Anyone intrepid enough to wish to attempt it at home will find a recipe in Escoffier's *Guide to Modern Cookery*. His ingredients include 4 lb of onions, 3 lb of carrots, 2 lb of leeks, 2 quarts of cider and ½ pint of Calvados or brandy besides the four feet and practically the whole stomach of the ox. And it is highly advisable, having eaten your *tripes à la mode*, to follow the Norman custom of drinking a *trou Normand*, or glass of Calvados, as a digestive before going on to the next course. One might think there wouldn't be a next course, but one would be mistaken. An important meal in this region, says Curnonsky in a guide to eating in Normandy, is always arranged thus: '*bouillon* and *pot-au-feu*, after which a glass of wine is taken; then tripe; then leg of mutton. Here a halt is called for the *trou Normand*. We fall to again with 11 roast veal, then fowl, then the desserts, coffee, and again Calvados.' This was pre-1939, and a mere snack compared with the lunch described by George Musgrave seventy years earlier in a travel book about Normandy (*A Ramble Through Normandy*, 1855). He watched a couple (on their honeymoon, he thought) on board the river steamer at Rouen consuming a midday meal of soup, fried mackerel, beefsteak, French beans and fried potatoes, an omelette *fines herbes*, a *fricandeau* of veal with sorrel, a roast chicken garnished with mushrooms, a hock of ham served upon spinach. There followed an apricot tart, three custards, and an endive salad, which were the precursors of a small roast leg of lamb, with chopped onion and nutmeg sprinkled upon it. Then came coffee and two glasses of absinthe, and *eau dorée*, a Mignon cheese, pears, plums, grapes and cakes. Two bottles of Burgundy and one of Chablis were emptied between eleven and one o'clock.

The True Emulsion

from *An Omelette and a Glass of Wine*

With the mayonnaise season in full blast, once more the familiar complaints about bottled mayonnaise and salad creams are heard in the land. Perhaps there is less cause for grumbling, thanks to the advent of the electric mixer combined with the whackings of the Postgate guide, than there used to be. The defence, when complaints are made, can no longer be that kitchen labour is lacking; it is simply the old one about the majority of customers preferring the synthetic product to the real thing. I am sure that this is very often perfectly true. Why?

Partly, the trouble lies in the characteristic English custom – which in some degree we share with the Swiss – of appropriating the *names* of established French and other foreign dishes, even of our own traditional ones, and attaching to them recipes of our own devising, often with the most carefree disregard of the ingredients and methods of cooking which made these dishes famous. The caterers, the manufacturers and the recipe-hashers employed by public relations firms to help sell factory products may reply that as long as a dish is found acceptable and sells it surely doesn't matter what it is called. Maybe these operators don't realize that what they are doing is fraudulent;

legally it isn't. There is no international patent or copyright law to protect the names or the recipes of recognized
traditional and classic dishes. While nobody in this country
can now, say, label any wine champagne that is not
champagne or pass off margarine as butter without risk of
prosecution, anybody depraved enough to invent a dish
consisting of a wedge of steam-heated bread spread with
tomato paste and a piece of synthetic Cheddar can call it
a pizza; for that matter they could sell a pizza as a Welsh
Rabbit and a Welsh Rabbit as a Swiss fondue or a *quiche
lorraine*; they can publish recipes for a soup called vichy-
ssoise containing everything and anything but what its
creator actually put into it – leeks and potatoes. At the
time the deceptions seem just sad or silly, but the conse-
quences can be far-reaching.

In the case of mayonnaise the damage may have been
done by the commercial firms and their bottled products
which were already on sale by the mid-1880s, but the
cookery advisers and experts certainly helped the public to
accept the name 'mayonnaise' as applied to a cooked
custard-type sauce made of flour, milk, eggs, and a very
high proportion of vinegar. Plenty of relevant recipes are
to be found in cookery books and other publications of the
period. Two examples will suffice. In the November 1895
issue of the *Epicure* magazine, under the heading 'New
Recipes', Miss Ida Cameron, principal of the Earls Court
Cookery School, contributed a recipe for what she called

cornflour mayonnaise. The lady explained that in this cooked mixture the cornflour 'does for thickening the sauce instead of salad oil'. Presumably this is what she was teaching her pupils. Herman Senn, a professional of very high standing, at one time chef to the Reform Club, author of countless cookery books, honorary secretary to the Universal Food and Cookery Association, editor of that body's magazine and promoter of a number of commercial products including one called Hygienic Caviar, was employed by Ward, Lock and Co. to edit the gigantic 1906 edition of Mrs Beeton. This edition contains two mayonnaise recipes. (Mrs Beeton's own original formula which had been left untouched for over forty years was dropped, one might think none too soon. It specified four tablespoons of vinegar to six of oil.) One of Senn's recipes was the authentic one, but called for a pint of olive oil to two eggs, an unnecessarily large allowance, tricky to work and, in view of the national English fear and dislike of olive oil, to which every cookery writer of the period refers and which was certainly a factor in the public's easy acceptance of the custard-type dressing in place of true mayonnaise, rather tactless. The second recipe Senn called 'cooked mayonnaise'. With his training he should surely have known that mayonnaise, whatever the origin of the word, had long been accepted in France, Spain and Italy as denoting an emulsion sauce of uncooked egg yolks and olive oil, and that the term 'cooked' used in conjunction with mayonnaise was contradictory.

As things turned out, the recipes from this 1906 edition were the ones which were finally established and accepted as Mrs Beeton's. From 1906 until the mid-1950s they were current – and of course much copied by other writers. During long periods of that half-century it is obvious that desperate shortages made Senn's pint of olive oil (one sees how it was that poor Mrs B. acquired her reputation for reckless extravagance) as ordered for the genuine recipe quite unpractical. And then, when even milk was scarce, why bother with the cooked version which orders a quarter of a pint of vinegar to half a pint of milk when it isn't all that much of an improvement on the mayonnaise or salad cream of commerce? (Although of course the ingredients of these products are not exactly as straightforward as Senn's were.) One has to remember that all this took place at a time when plain English cooks reigned in the majority of English kitchens. They followed plain English recipes and chiefly those from the Mrs Beeton books or their derivatives. Few of them or their employers experimented or questioned what the books said. By the thirties there was already a vast public brought up in the belief that mayonnaise was a sauce which could only be produced in a factory, which contained no olive oil – and tasted mainly of acetic acid. And that is what, by the sixties, when they see mayonnaise announced on a menu, the great majority of people expect. It is not unnatural that they should be suspicious and indignant when confronted with the authentic sauce. Like most tastes, that for olive oil and mayonnaise made with it is an acquired one. Those of us who have acquired it, and hold that the original version of mayonnaise is the only true one, also feel that we should be entitled to accuse the caterer who offers us something totally different under the same name, of fraudulent practice. The caterer is the inheritor of the confusions created by our own indifference to the composition of any given dish so long as it bears an attractive name.

The Spectator, 3 August 1962

AÏOLI

from *French Provincial Cooking*

Provençal *aïoli* – dish of the farmhouse and the *cabanon* [hut belonging to a *gardian* of the Camargue] – triumph of the Provençal kitchen, is composed of a garlic mayonnaise and an assortment, as varied as possible, of fresh vegetables cooked in salted water, white fish cooked in *court-bouillon* and cold meats.

EUGÈNE BLANCARD, *Mets de Provence*, 1926

Aïoli is indeed one of the most famous and most beloved of all Provençal dishes. The magnificent shining golden ointment which is the sauce is often affectionately referred

17

to as the 'butter of Provence'. With this wonderful sauce are served boiled salt cod, potatoes, beetroot, sweet peppers, either raw or cooked, carrots, a fine boiled fish such as a bream or mullet, hard-boiled eggs, sometimes little inkfish or octopus, French beans, globe artichokes, even little snails and perhaps a salad of chick peas.

The *aïoli garni* is, in fact, a Friday dish as well as one of the traditional Christmas Eve dishes; on non-fasting days the beef from the *pot-au-feu* or even a boiled chicken may form part of the dish: it then becomes *le grand aïoli*. It will be seen, then, that with all these different accompaniments, the *aïoli garni* is essentially a dish for a large family or a party of intimate friends, although personally I could quite well dispense with all the rest provided there were a large bowl of potatoes boiled in their skins and perhaps some raw peppers and celery to go with the *aïoli*. In a small country restaurant in Provence where I once asked, at short notice, if it were possible to produce an *aïoli garni* for dinner, it was too late for the *patron* to go out and buy anything specially, but he produced a handsome dish of ham accompanied by potatoes and the vegetables in season, with the *aïoli* in a bowl in the centre of the dish. It was an excellent demonstration of the sort of impromptu *aïoli* which can be produced with ingredients to hand.

Allow roughly 2 large cloves of garlic per person and, for eight people, the yolks of 3 eggs and nearly a pint of very good quality olive oil – failing Provençal olive oil, the best Italian or Spanish will do. Crush the peeled garlic in a mortar until it is reduced absolutely to pulp. Add the yolks and a pinch of salt. Stir with a wooden spoon. When the eggs and garlic are well amalgamated, start adding the oil, very slowly at first, drop by drop, until the *aïoli* begins to thicken. This takes longer than with a straightforward mayonnaise because the garlic has thinned the yolks to a certain extent. When about half the oil has been used, the *aïoli* should be a very thick mass, and the oil can now be added in a slow but steady stream. The sauce gets thicker and thicker, and this is as it should be; a good *aïoli* is practically solid. Add a very little lemon juice at the end, and serve the sauce either in the kitchen mortar in which you have made it or piled up in a small salad bowl. Should the *aïoli* separate through the oil having been added too fast, put a fresh yolk into another bowl and gradually add the curdled mixture to it. The *aïoli* then comes back to life.

Now as to the amount of garlic: you can, of course, use less but you are likely to find that the mass of eggs and oil is then too heavy and rich. A true *aïoli* is a remarkable 19 mixture of the smooth mayonnaise combined with the powerful garlic flavour which tingles in your throat as you swallow it. One Provençal writer suggests that those who find the *aïoli* indigestible should take a *trou* or *coup du milieu* in the form of a little glass of *marc* in the middle of the meal.

Picnics

from *Summer Cooking*

Picnic addicts seem to be roughly divided between those who frankly make elaborate preparations and leave nothing to chance, and those others whose organization is no less complicated but who are more deceitful and pretend that everything will be obtained on the spot and cooked over a woodcutter's fire, conveniently to hand; there are even those, according to Richard Jefferies, who wisely take the precaution of visiting the site of their intended picnic some days beforehand and there burying the champagne.

Not long before the war I was staying with friends in Marseille. One Saturday night a picnic was arranged for the next day with some American acquaintances; it was agreed that the two parties should proceed in their own cars to a little bay outside Marseille, and that we should each bring our own provisions. On Sunday morning I and my friends indulged in a delicious hour of shopping in the wonderful market of the rue de Rome, buying olives, anchovies, salame sausages, pâtés, yards of bread, smoked fish, fruit and cheese. With a provision of cheap red wine we bundled the food into the car and set off, stopping now and again for a drink; so that we arrived at our rendezvous well disposed to appreciate the sun, the sea and the scent of wild herbs and Mediterranean pines. Presently our friends drove up and started to unload their car. One of the first things to come out was a hatchet, with which they efficiently proceeded to chop down olive branches, and in no time at all there was a blazing fire. Out of their baskets came cutlets, potatoes, bacon, skewers, frying pans, jars of ice, butter, tablecloths, all the trappings of a minor barbecue. Our reactions as we watched these proceedings were those of astonishment, admiration, and finally, as realization of the inadequacy of our own catering dawned, dismay. How wilted they seemed, those little packets wrapped up in rather oily paper; the olives which had glowed with colour in the market stalls of the rue de Rome looked shabby now; the salame seemed dried up and the anchovies a squalid mess. Miserably, like poor relations, we sat with our shameful bundles spread out on the grass and politely offered them to our friends. They were kind, but obviously preferred their own grilled cutlets and fried potatoes, and we were too embarrassed to accept their proffered hospitality. Presently they produced ice cream out of a thermos, but by now we were past caring, and finally it was their turn for surprise when they found we hadn't even provided ourselves with the means of making a cup of coffee.

Then there was the hospitable family I remember in my childhood; they owned a beautiful house and an elegant garden and were much given to out-of-door entertainments, pageants and picnics. On picnic days a large party of children and grown-ups would be assembled in the hall. Led by our host and hostess we proceeded through the exquisite formal Dutch garden, across the lane and over a fence into a coppice. Close on our heels followed the butler, the chauffeur and the footman, bearing fine china plates, the silver and tablecloths, and a number of vast dishes containing cold chickens, jellies and trifles. Arrived at the end of our journey, five minutes from the house, our host set about making a fire, with sticks which I suspect had been strategically placed by the gardener, over which we grilled quantities of sausages and bacon, which were devoured amidst the customary jokes and hilarity. The picnickers' honour thus satisfied, we took our places for an orderly meal, handed round by the footman, and in composition resembling that of an Edwardian wedding breakfast.

Since those days I have had a good many opportunities of evolving a picnic technique on the lines laid down by Henry James, 'not so good as to fail of an amusing disorder, nor yet so bad as to defeat the proper function of repasts'.

Before deciding upon the food, its packing and transport must be planned. (I am assuming for the moment a car-transported picnic.) Those who are lucky enough to possess an Edwardian picnic hamper, fitted with spirit lamp and kettle, sandwich tins and a variety of boxes and bottles, need look no further. These hampers may be cumbersome, but they are capacious and solid; an aura of lavish gallivantings and ancient Rolls-Royces hangs about them, and they are infinitely superior to the modern kind in which the use of every inch of space has been planned for you in advance. (At the Lord Roberts workshop in the Brompton Road there are deep square baskets of very solid construction, large enough to hold a good deal of food as well as several bottles, which are still very reasonable in price. This establishment is full of happy ideas for all addicts of eating out of doors, for they sell large hampers, unfitted, so that you can pack whatever you please, baskets with divisions for bottles, baskets for thermos jars, and the most comfortable garden chairs in existence.) Insulated picnic bags are highly effective and useful.

As to plates and glasses, if I am going to have them at all I would prefer to have china plates and glass glasses, although it must be admitted that clear, colourless plastic glasses such as are used on airlines are more practical.

A spirit lamp and kettle plus a tin of Nescafé provide a hotter and fresher cup of coffee than any which ever came out of a vacuum flask. Iced coffee on the other hand can be transported in thermos jugs, and a large thermos jar filled with ice is a blessing for those who don't care for warm drinks, or who like to put ice into coarse red picnic wine.

As for the food, the buying and preparing of it always

seem to me to provide half the fun. The possibilities are almost without limit. On the whole, though, I think that such elegant foods as foie gras and lobster patties should be excluded as they seem to lose their fine lustre when eaten out of doors, whereas the simpler charms of salame sausage, fresh cheese, black olives and good French bread (if you can find such a commodity) are enhanced when they are eaten on the hillside or the seashore. Sandwiches I rather like (George Saintsbury considered that venison makes the best sandwiches), but many people do not, so there must always be alternatives; thin slices of ham rolled round Frankfurter sausages, or Frankfurter sausages split in half enclosing a slice of Gruyère cheese are good ones. Remember that such delicious foods as jellied egg, duck in aspic, and so on aren't really ideal for long journeys on a hot day because the jelly (if it has been made as it should be) will melt *en route*; mayonnaise also has a dismaying habit of turning into a rather unappetizing-looking oily mass when the weather is hot. A cold chicken with a cream sauce is a better bid than a chicken mayonnaise. Cold steak and kidney pudding is fine picnic food, so is cold spiced beef, which cuts into nice slices. Cold escalopes of veal, fried in egg and breadcrumbs, make excellent picnic food provided they are very thin and very well drained after frying. Hard-boiled eggs are time-honoured picnic food, so I always take a few, but they are not everybody's taste. Cheese seems to me essential for an   25 out-of-doors meal; next to the salty little Mediterranean goat's and sheep's milk cheeses English Cheddar or Cheshire, or Gruyère, are perhaps the easiest picnic cheeses. Some people like a rich moist fruit cake for a picnic, but I prefer a slab of the driest, bitterest chocolate available (Terry's make a good one but the best is the Belgian Côte d'Or), to be eaten in alternate mouthfuls with a Marie biscuit. Apples and figs and apricots, because they are easy to eat and transport as well as being good in the open air, are perhaps the best fruit for a picnic.

The nicest drinks for picnics are the obvious ones. A stout red wine such as a Macon or a Chianti, which cannot be unduly harmed by the journey in the car; vin rosé (particularly delicious by the sea); cider, lager, shandy, Black Velvet; iced sherry and bitters. For a very hot day Pimm's No 1 couldn't be bettered but involves some organization in the matter of cucumber, lemonade, oranges, mint, borage, and all the paraphernalia, and a thermos jar of ice is essential. An effective way to keep wine and mineral waters cool on a long journey is to wrap the bottles in several sheets of dampened newspaper.

For soft drinks the most refreshing are tinned grapefruit, orange or pineapple juice, and tomato juice. (In this case include the tin opener.) Delicate china tea, iced, with slices of lemon and mint leaves is admirably reviving. An early edition of Mrs Beeton asserts that 'Water can usually 26 be obtained so it is useless to take it.' For the walker's picnic perhaps the perfect meal has been described by Sir Osbert Sitwell: 'the fruits of the month, cheese with the goaty taste of mountains upon it, and if possible bilberries, apples, raw celery, a meal unsophisticated and pastoral . . .'

Juanita's Tortilla

from *A Book of Mediterranean Food*

The first time I ever visited Spain, in 1964, I stayed with Anthony Denney, the photographer and interior decorator who was later to create both the wonderfully simple black-and-white decor for my kitchen utensil shop and the extraordinary window displays which remained unique of their kind – however many people copied the merchandise I sold in my shop, and many did, nobody was capable of imitating Anthony's window dressing.

Anthony's Spanish house was in the province of Alicante, high up in the hills close to the little village of Finestrat. At the time, two local girls, Mercedes and Juanita, looked after the house and prepared the meals. Most of the cooking was done by Mercedes, the elder one, but now and then seventeen-year-old Juanita took over. Her *tortilla* was memorable. We used to take one on picnics, and even on car journeys of several days a *tortilla* was a valuable standby for our midday meals – it was by no means to be taken for granted that we would always find an inn or a restaurant on our route.

One day as Juanita made her *tortilla*, I noted down just how she prepared and cooked it.

Allow about 1 lb of potatoes for 4 eggs.

The peeled potatoes all to be cut up small; then soaked in plenty of water (as for a gratin dauphinois).

They are cooked in olive oil – Juanita heats it until it smokes – in a shallow earthenware dish placed directly over the gas. She adds a tiny piece of garlic, and stirs the potatoes fairly often, pressing them down with the typical Spanish iron spatula-spoon. Season with salt. In the end the potatoes become almost a cohered mass. If any of the pieces are too large Juanita cuts them as they cook with her iron implement. Having transferred the cooked potatoes to a bowl so that they cool a little, Juanita beats the eggs in another bowl, flings in the potatoes.

In an omelette pan she heats oil until it smokes. She throws in the eggs and potatoes. The mixture puffs up. In her left hand Juanita holds a deep plate. Into this she turns the *tortilla*. Then she slides it back into the pan. She repeats the process, sometimes twice. It depends if she is satisfied with the appearance of the *tortilla*.

This *tortilla* should come out like a cake, quite thick, so you mustn't use too large a pan for frying it.

Most Spanish cooks put onions in their *tortillas* but I prefer Juanita's version, with just that small touch of garlic.

Golden Delicious

from *An Omelette and a Glass of Wine*

As Sunday lunches go in the village hotels of the Vaucluse department of Provence, the meal we had in the Hostellerie du Château at Beaumes de Venise was far from a bad one. Memorable it was not, except for two points neither of them relevant to the cooking and and one of which has only now, seven years later, become manifest.

It was the early summer of 1956. The calamitous frosts of the previous winter and spring had wrought havoc with the countryside which was fearful to see. The slopes and valleys of the Vaucluse and of all that country east and north-east of Avignon to Cavaillon, Apt, Pernes-les-Fontaines, Le Thor and Carpentras, which was once the papal county of Venaissin, should have been silver and freshly grey-green in the early June sun. The whole landscape was gashed with ugly black wounds. Hundreds of olive trees, withered and blighted by the frosts and the all-blasting mistral winds which followed them, had been cut down or were standing like ancient skeletons in that fertile and beflowered landscape which is the heart and core of Provence. The tall rows of dark cypress trees, windbreaks against the destroying mistral, were unnecessary reminders

that life in Provence is not always quite so idyllic as it may look to two English visitors driving one Sunday morning in early June from Malaucène near the foot of the Mont Ventoux toward a village so irresistibly named Beaumes de Venise. For the odd thing was that after we had lost our way three times in the identical piece of country, it dawned upon us that this piece of country *was* idyllic, almost too good to be true. In this pocket of land apparently untouched by the ravaging winter were no scars, no dead or doomed trees. The olives were bright with life and thick with young leaves. The crippled landscape was here restored and complete.

It was perhaps the sense of relief that somewhere at least in Provence that year there would be an olive crop and peasant farmers whose livelihoods had not been utterly destroyed that made Beaumes de Venise, when eventually we reached it, rather less interesting than the little piece of country we had passed through on our way. Subsequent inquiries revealed that the olives and the olive oil of Beaumes de Venise have a substantial local reputation; and we did, I remember, remark upon the excellence of the salad and upon an unusual anchovy-flavoured, oil-based sauce offered with the routine Sunday roast chicken that day at lunch. Nothing extraordinary about that. In this region, salads with good olive oil dressings, and mayonnaise sauces tasting perceptibly of fruity oil are, or were in the days before the frost destruction, the rule rather than the exception as they are in Northern France. 31

As for the wine, I do not remember what we drank. Probably it was that reliable wine of Provence restaurants, red Gigondas from the vineyards north of Beaumes on the far side of the Dentelles de Montmirail. The wine we did not drink was, as it turned out, the remarkable one. We did not drink it because we had never heard of it, and if it was on the wine list of the hotel – which according to Michelin it now is – we did not notice it.

The wine of Beaumes de Venise is a natural sweet golden wine made from muscat grapes with their own appellation of *Muscat de Beaumes* and unmixed with the Hamburg muscat which coarsens many of the sweet wines of Provence. Nobody, it seems, quite knows when the muscat grapes of Beaumes de Venise were first planted nor how the sweet wine from the vineyards of this tiny area protected by a fold in the hills from the savage north winds acquired its reputation. Certainly that reputation has always been a local one only. There are no more than three or four hectares under vine cultivation, a production of two hundred hectolitres a year and only two growers. From one of these growers, M. Combres, Mr Gerald Asher of the firm of Asher, Storey and Co., 127 Lower Thames Street, EC1, to whose admirable sense of enterprise we already owe the import of so many interesting French regional wines hitherto unknown or unobtainable in this country, has bought the muscat wine of Beaumes de Venise. It is, I believe, the first time this wine has ever been exported. As far as I am concerned its journey was worthwhile.

The custom of drinking a little glass of rich wine with a sweet dish or fruit seems to me a civilized one, and especially welcome to those who do not or cannot swig brandy or port after a meal. The great dessert wines of Bordeaux and the Rhine are rather beyond the reach of ordinary mortals and are in any case wines which demand a certain ceremony. Your meal has to work up to them. The wine of Beaumes, although so rare, seems somehow more within the scope of the simplest or even of an improvised meal. It retails at about 22s. a bottle, which seems reasonable enough since an opened bottle, securely recorked, appears to remain in good condition for some while. A few days ago I shared with a friend the final glasses from a bottle opened before Christmas. With it we ate a fresh apricot tart. The musky golden wine of Beaumes – according to Mr Asher, and I see no reason to quarrel with his judgement, 'its bouquet is penetrating and flower-like, its flavour both honey-sweet and tangy' – and the sweet apricots, vanilla-sugared on crumbly pastry, made an original and entrancing combination of food and wine.

Why Venise? What balm or balsam in conjunction with what lakes, lagoons, canals? Neither and none. The name Venise, they say, has the same origin as Venaissin and Vénasque, that ancient and rather forlorn little village perched on an escarpment overlooking the twisting road between Carpentras and the Forest of Murs. All, it is supposed, stem from *aveniensis* or *avignonnais*. Beaumes is not balm or balsam. In the Provençal language *baumo* is a grotto. The Vaucluse country is honeycombed with caves and grottoes, many of them used for the cultivation of mushrooms. As a spectacle one set of holes in a rock is, I find, much the same as another. So that day we took it on trust from the *Guide Bleu* that the cliffs at the back of the village of Beaumes are '*percées de grottes*'. Still, it is not unpleasing to learn that the meaning of *baumanière*, as in the super-glossy three-star Hostellerie de Baumanière below Les Baux, is really *baume a niero*, in French *grotto à puces*, the grotto of the fleas.

The Spectator, 10 January 1964

The dessert wine of Beaumes de Venise is now exported in quantity to Britain and the United States. Sometimes I wish it had not become so popular. At any rate I would advise avoidance of the product of that grower who bottles his wine in very fancy cordial bottles.

Italian Dishes in Foreign Kitchens

from *Italian Food*

The difficulties of reproducing Italian cooking abroad are much the same as the difficulties attendant upon any good cooking outside its country of origin, and usually they can be overcome.

Italians, unlike the thrifty French, are very extravagant with raw materials. Butter, cheese, oil, the best cuts of meat, chicken and turkey breasts, eggs, chicken and meat broth, raw and cooked ham are used not so much with reckless abandon as with a precise awareness of what good quality does for the cooking.

In most Italian households the marketing is done twice a day. Everything is freshly cooked for every meal. What the Italian kitchen misses in the form of concentrated meat glazes, *fumets* of fish and game, the *fonds de cuisine* of the French, it makes up for in the extreme freshness and lavishness of its raw materials. It is worth bearing in mind that when an Italian has not the wherewithal to cook one of the traditional extravagant dishes she doesn't attempt to produce an imitation. No amount of propaganda could persuade her to see the point of making, let us say, a steak and kidney pudding with tinned beef and no kidneys, neither would she bother to make a ravioli stuffing with leftovers, because the results would not at all resemble the dish as it should be, and would therefore be valueless. So her method would be to produce some attractive and nourishing little dish out of two ounces of cheese and a slice of ham, or a pound of spinach and a couple of eggs. A hefty *pizza* made of bread dough and baked in the oven with tomatoes, cheese and herbs costs very little and is comforting, savoury food. *Gnocchi* made of potatoes, or of semolina flour, or of spinach and *ricotta* (fresh white sheep's [or cow's] milk cheese), are cheap and easy to make, so are little envelopes of paste containing slices of cheese and *mortadella* sausage, and *mozzarella in carrozza*, a fried cheese sandwich. Because Parmesan cheese is expensive, many people eat their spaghetti in the rough-and-ready but extremely good Neapolitan way, with olive oil and garlic. From such methods I believe we could learn much of value from the Italians. Not that Italian cookery is without its faults. The excessive use of cheese, the too frequent appearance of tomato sauce, the over-working of the frying pan (expert as Italian cooks are with it), too heavy a hand with powerful herbs, are some of the points at which fault could be found with the Italian kitchen.

There is no reason, however, why we should not combine the best which it has to offer (and the best in Italy is extremely good) with materials at our disposal in this country. The number of different ways of making use, for example, of a small quantity of veal is astounding. (I have given a dozen such recipes in this book, and there are plenty more.) We could benefit from Italian methods of frying and grilling fish; and as we have not one single fish soup in common use in this country, could we not invent one? Again, once the delicate flavour of genuine Bolognese or Parma stuffings for *anolini* or *cappelletti* have been compared with the coarse mixtures contained in bought ravioli, the idea of making these things at home cannot fail to appeal.

The delicacy and intrinsic goodness of the simplest white *risotto* eaten only with Parmesan cheese and good fresh butter will also quickly be appreciated. Tied as we are by tradition in the matter of the roast turkey, we complain that it is a dull and dry bird, but continue to eat it cooked in the same way; the Italian fashion of cooking the breast with butter, ham and cheese will be a revelation. Home-made cream cheese can be turned to good account in twenty different dishes in the Italian manner. To make *pasta* at home may sound a formidable undertaking, but if any Italian peasant girl can make it without effort we should presumably be able, after two or three attempts, to master the technique. And now of course pasta machines, whether hand-operated or electrically powered, are easily obtainable.

Some interesting sidelights emerge from a study of Italian cooking. The beautiful colours of their food is one 37 most characteristic point. The vivid scarlet dishes of the south, the tomato sauce and the pimentos, the oranges and pinks of fish soups, the red and white of a Neapolitan *pizza*, contrast strikingly with the unique green food of central and northern Italy; the spinach *gnocchi* of Tuscany, the *lasagne verdi* of Bologna, the green *pesto* sauce of Genoa, the green peas and rice of the Veneto, green artichokes in pies, in omelettes, in salads; the green and yellow marbled stuffings of rolled beef and veal dishes – such food can scarcely fail to charm. Then there is the point of the endless hours Italian cooks are willing to spend over the pounding of intricate stuffings and sauces, and the startling rapidity with which the actual cooking is carried out (five minutes in boiling water for the ravioli, into the frying pan and out with the *polpette*, the *crocchette* and the *frittelle* which have been most patiently chopped, sieved, and rolled out on the pastry board).

The seemingly deliberate misunderstanding by French cooks of Italian food is another curious point. 'Two table-spoons of rice for a *risotto* for four'; 'the Milanese like their rice half-cooked' – one reads with astonishment such instructions from otherwise irreproachable French cookery books. Ali-Bab, in his monumental work *Gastronomie Pratique*, falls into the common trap of asserting that 'poultry and butcher's meats are (in Italy) frankly mediocre', and 'the most common vegetables are broccoli and fennel'. It is scarcely to be wondered at that in their turn a good many Italians just jeer at French cooking (French dishes are rarely well cooked in Italy), although they make a mistake in deriding the slowly simmered, patiently amalgamated dishes of wine, meat, and vegetables which play such an important part in the marvellous regional food of France. There *are* long-cooked meat dishes in the Italian kitchen, and soups containing haricot beans or chick peas which must be cooked for several hours; but on the whole Italian cooks neither like nor understand these methods. As I have already sufficiently explained, quality and freshness of flavour are the all-important elements in Italian cooking; and in describing the dishes in this book I have deviated as little as possible from the correct ingredients and quantities, so that the food may retain its authentic flavour.

PESTO

One large bunch of fresh basil, garlic, a generous ounce each of pine nuts and grated Sardo or Parmesan cheese, $1\frac{1}{2}$–2 oz of olive oil.

Pound the basil leaves (there should be about 2 oz when the stalks have been removed) in a mortar with 1 or 2 cloves of garlic, a little salt and the pine nuts. Add the cheese. (Sardo cheese is the pungent Sardinian ewe's milk cheese which is exported in large quantities to Genoa to make *pesto*. Parmesan and Sardo are sometimes used in equal quantities, or all Parmesan, which gives the *pesto* a milder flavour.)

When the *pesto* is a thick purée start adding the olive oil, a little at a time. Stir it steadily and see that it is amalgamating with the other ingredients, as the finished sauce should have the consistency of a creamed butter. If made in larger quantities *pesto* may be stored in jars, covered with a layer of olive oil.

This is the famous sauce which is eaten by the Genoese with all kinds of *pasta*, with *gnocchi*, and as a flavouring for soups. The Genoese claim that their basil has a far superior flavour to that grown in any other part of Italy, and assert that a good *pesto* can only be made with Genoese basil. As made in Genoa it is certainly one of the best sauces yet invented for *pasta*, and 1 tablespoon of *pesto* stirred in at the last minute gives a most delicious flavour to a *minestrone*. Try it also with baked potatoes instead of butter.

Since basil is not easy to find in England except for people who grow it themselves, an imitation of this sauce can be made with parsley, and although the flavour is totally different it is still very good indeed – although it cannot of course be called *pesto*. Walnuts can be used instead of pine nuts.

There are various versions of *risotto alla Milanese*. The classic one is made simply with chicken broth and flavoured with saffron; butter and grated Parmesan cheese are stirred in at the end of the cooking, and more cheese and butter served with it. The second version is made with beef marrow and white wine; a third with Marsala. In each case saffron is used as a flavouring.

Risotto is such a simple and satisfactory dish, so universally appreciated, that it is well worth mastering the principles of cooking the rice, after which any amount of different dishes can be improvised. It can be served absolutely plain with butter and cheese, or it can be elaborated with the addition of chicken, duck, game, lobster, mussels, oysters, prawns, mushrooms, truffles, goose or chicken livers, artichoke hearts, peas, aubergines, almost anything you like. But not more than one or two of such ingredients in one *risotto*.

For *risotto alla Milanese* with white wine, proceed as follows: into a heavy pan put a good ounce of butter (in northern Italy butter is always used for *risotto*, in the south it is very often made with oil). In the butter fry a small onion cut very fine; let it turn pale gold but not brown; then add 1 oz of beef marrow extracted from marrow bones; this gives a richer quality to the *risotto*, but 41 can perfectly well be left out. Now add the rice, allowing about 3 oz per person (in Italy they would allow a good deal more; the amount rather depends upon whether the *risotto* is to constitute a first course only or a main dish). Stir the rice until it is well impregnated with the butter. It must remain white. Now pour in two thirds of a tumbler of dry white wine and let it cook on a moderate flame until the wine has almost evaporated. At this moment start adding the stock, which should be a light chicken consommé and which is kept barely simmering in another pan; add about a breakfastcupful (in American terms, a regular measuring cup) at a time, and keep your eye on the *risotto*, although at this stage it is not essential to stir continuously. As the stock becomes absorbed add more; in all you will need about 2 pints for 10–12 oz of rice, and if this is not quite enough, dilute it with hot water. Towards the end of the cooking, which will take 20–30 minutes, stir continuously using a wooden fork rather than a spoon, which tends to crush the grains. When you see that the rice is tender, the mixture creamy but not sticky, add the saffron.

The proper way to do this is to pound the filaments to a powder (three or four will be enough for 12 oz of rice), steep the powder in a coffee cupful of the broth for 5 minutes, and strain the liquid obtained into the rice. Having stirred in the saffron, add 1 oz each of butter and grated Parmesan, and serve the *risotto* as soon as the cheese has melted. More butter and grated cheese must be served separately.

To make *risotto* with Marsala, proceed in exactly the same way, omitting the beef marrow, which would make too rich a combination, and using only half a glass of Marsala.

RISO ALLA GENOVESE

This is a rice dish cooked by a different method from that used for the classic *risotto*.

First of all prepare the following sauce: 8 oz of raw minced beef or veal, 3 or 4 carrots, a half head of celery, a large onion, seasonings, herbs, and $\frac{1}{4}$ pint of white wine. Sauté the chopped vegetables in hot butter or oil or a mixture of the two; let them turn golden but not brown; add the meat and stir it until it has browned a little, then pour in the wine; let this reduce by half and then cover the pan; leave it to simmer for an hour, until the sauce is syrupy.

In the meantime boil 12–16 oz of rice in a very large pan of boiling salted water; let it be very slightly under-done (about 12 minutes, but the exact time must depend upon the quality of the rice). Drain it very thoroughly, put it into a clean pan, and shake it over a low flame so that it dries. At this stage pour in half the sauce and a small lump of butter; stir it for 5 minutes over a low fire, turn it out on to a dish, and pour the rest of the sauce over it. Grated cheese is served separately.

Chez *Barattero*

from *An Omelette and a Glass of Wine*

From 1956 to 1961 I contributed a monthly cookery article to London *Vogue*. In those days cookery writers were very minor fry. Expenses were perks paid to photographers, fashion editors and other such exalted personages. Foreign currency allowances were severely restricted, so cookery contributors didn't come in for subsidised jaunts to Paris or marathons round three star eating cathedrals. They were supposed to supply their articles out of some inexhaustible well of knowledge and their ingredients out of their own funds. At a monthly fee of £20 an article (increased at some stage, I think, to £25) it was quite a struggle to keep up the flow of properly tested recipes, backed up with informative background material, local colour and general chatter. So it was with gratitude that one year I accepted an offer from my editor, the original and enlightened Audrey Withers, to go on the occasional trip to France, provided with £100 from Condé Nast to help cover restaurant meals, hotels, petrol and so on. To be sure, £100 wasn't exactly princely even in those days, but it was double the ordinary currency allowance, and even though those trips were very much France on a shoestring, the knowledge I derived from them was 45 valuable. In French provincial restaurants at that time local and regional dishes weren't always double-priced on a 'menu touristique'. Some, incredible as it now seems, would be listed as a matter of course on the everyday menus of quite ordinary restaurants. Asked nicely, a *patron* might come up with a speciality based, say, on some local farmhouse pork product, or on a cheese peculiar to the immediate district, perhaps an omelette of the chef's own devising, or a simple fish dish with an uncommon sauce. It was for ideas and stimulus that I was looking, not restaurant set pieces.

On one trip, however, I came to make the acquaintance of Madame Barattero and her Hôtel du Midi at Lamastre in the Ardèche. Now, a hotel with a Michelin two-star restaurant attached might not seem exactly the appropriate choice for people on a restricted budget. As things turned out, that particular two-star restaurant-hotel proved, in the long run, very much cheaper, infinitely better value, and far more rewarding than most of the technically cheap places we'd found. Staying at Lamastre on half-pension terms was restful and comfortable. Every day we drove out to the countryside, usually taking a picnic, or lunching at a small town or village restaurant. In the evening we were provided by Madame Barattero with a delicious dinner made up of quite simple dishes geared to the price charged to *pensionnaires*. Prime ingredients and skilled cooking were, however, very much included in our *en pension* terms. That lesson was a valuable one, and seemed well worth passing on to my readers.

My account of the Hôtel du Midi was published in *Vogue* in September 1958. I should add that while much of the material published in *Vogue* as a result of my trips to France in the fifties was incorporated in *French Provincial Cooking*, this was one of several articles which got away. There did not seem to be a place for it in the book, and in fact it was, in its day, unique for a *Vogue* food article in that it included no recipes. It was, again, Audrey Withers who took the decision to publish an article quite unorthodox by the rules prevailing at the time. I appreciated her imaginative gesture. With Madame Barattero I remained on friendly terms for many years, receiving a moving welcome every time I visited her hotel. Two years ago, after a brief retirement, Madame Barattero died. Her declining years had been clouded by increasing deafness, by the withdrawal of one of her Michelin stars, and I believe other untoward happenings. The restaurant of the Hôtel du Midi is now in the hands of the same chef who was in charge of the kitchens all those years ago, and who had long since become a partner in the business. I have not visited Lamastre for several years now, so cannot express any opinion on the cooking. I am glad though to be able to republish my article, as a tribute to Madame Barattero's memory.

Rose Barattero is the euphonious name of the proprietress of the Hôtel du Midi at Lamastre in the Ardèche. Slim, elegant, her pretty grey hair in tight curls all over her head, the minuscule red ribbon of the Legion of Honour on her grey dress, Madame Barattero is an impressive little figure as she stands on the terrace of her hotel welcoming her guests as they drive into the main square of the small provincial town whose name she has made famous throughout France.

Here, in this town, in the modest hotel which stands back to back with her own, she was born. Her parents were hotel keepers, her brother inherited, and still runs, the old Hôtel de la Poste. Her sister has a hotel at St-Vallier down on the Rhône. Her husband, a *niçois*, and a relation of the Escoffier family, started his career as an apprentice at the Carlton in London, and was already making a name for himself as a promising chef when she married him and they set up on their own at the Hôtel du Midi.

When M. Barattero died in 1941 the hotel was already celebrated for its cooking. His young widow took over the running of the hotel and the restaurant, putting the kitchen in the charge of a hard-working and modest chef who had started as Barattero's apprentice. His wife looks after the accounts and the reception work. During the past fifteen years or so the fame of Barattero's at Lamastre has spread throughout France; Madame Barattero's name is among the most respected in the entire French restaurant industry.

In the fiercely competitive world of the French catering business this is no ordinary achievement. Lamastre is a town of little over three thousand inhabitants. It is not on a main road; the country round about, although magnificent and infinitely varied, is not known to tourists in the way in which, let us say, Provence or the château country of the Loire are known, for there is not very much left in the way of architectural or historical interest for the ordinary sightseer. In other words, a place like Barattero's must rely, not on the local population and the passing tourist, but upon those customers who make the journey to Lamastre expressly for the cooking.

Michelin awards Madame Barattero two stars. Now, although Michelin one-star restaurants are very much on the chancy side, both as regards quality and price, and such of their three-star establishments (there are only eleven in the whole of France) into which I have penetrated, either a little too rarefied in atmosphere for my taste – or, as Raymond Mortimer observed recently of a famous Paris house, the food is too rich and so are the customers – it is rare to find the two-star places at fault. As far as the provinces are concerned these two-star establishments (there are fifty-nine of them in the whole country, about twenty of which are in Paris) offer very remarkable value. I do not mean to suggest that they are places for the impecunious, but rather that while the cooking which they have to offer is unique, the charges compare more than favourably with those prevailing in hundreds of other French establishments where the surroundings vary between the grandiose and the squalid and where the cooking, while probably sound enough, is uneven or without distinction.

I have often heard the criticism that these modest establishments of two-star quality, offering, as most of them do, no more than half a dozen specialities at most, are places whose resources are exhausted after a couple of meals, or alternatively that the accommodation which they have to offer is not up to the standard of the cooking. So tourists make their pilgrimage to eat a meal at a place like the Midi at Lamastre, the Chapon Fin at Thoissey, or the Armes de France at Ammerschwihr and move on without knowing that they could have stayed for several days, not only in comfort and quiet and enjoying a variety of beautifully cooked dishes, but quite often at considerably reduced prices for pension or half-pension terms.

Early last summer we drove from Lyon down the western bank of the Rhône towards St-Péray, and there turned off up the steep and beautiful road which leads to Lamastre and St-Agrève. We had been warned that the forty-odd kilometres from St-Péray to Lamastre would take us twice as long as we expected because of the sinuous road, so we had allowed plenty of time, and arrived in front of the Hôtel du Midi while the afternoon sun was still shining over the little *place*. Our welcome from Madame Barattero was so warm and the rooms we were shown so airy, light and sympathetically furnished, the bathroom so immense and shining, the little garden below our terrace so pretty and orderly, that we decided there and then to stay several days. We discussed half-pension terms with Madame and then made ourselves scarce until dinner time.

Now it must be explained that chez Barattero there are five special dishes for which the house is renowned. They are *galantine de caneton*, a *pain d'écrevisses sauce cardinal*, a *poularde en vessie*, a *saucisse en feuilletage* and a dish of artichoke hearts with a creamy sauce which they call *artichauts Escoffier*. If you were really trying you could, I suppose, taste them all at one meal (indeed four of them figure on the 1,800 franc menu, the most expensive one, the others being 1,600 and 1,200) but we could take our time and enjoy them gradually. We left the choice of our menus to Madame. Indeed, there was little alternative but to do so. For although she does not herself do the cooking Madame has been studying her guests and composing menus for them for thirty-four years and she neither likes being contradicted nor is capable of making a mistake in this respect. She knew without being told that we didn't want to overload ourselves with food, however delicious; with an unerring touch she provided us night after night with menus which I think it is worth describing if only to demonstrate one or two important points about French restaurant cooking. First, how varied the food can be even in a place where the advertised specialities are very limited; secondly, how well worth while it is eating even the simplest of the routine dishes of French cookery produced in an absolutely first-class manner. ('One does not come here to eat something as ordinary as *oeufs en gelée*,' the archbishop-like head waiter in a famous Paris restaurant once said to me. He was wrong. Such simple things are the test of a really good establishment.) And thirdly, how very much a good dish gains by being served quite on its own, without fussy garnish or heaps of vegetables to overfill you and to get in the way of your sauce, to distract from the main flavours of the chicken or the fish and to sicken you of the sight of food long before the end of the meal.

We could have started every meal with soup had we so wished, but in fact we did so only once or twice because they were so good that we should have eaten too much. And the last part of the meal always consisted of a fine platter of cheeses and either strawberries, cherries or an ice, so I will leave those items out of the following account of our menus.

The wines we drank were mostly recent Rhône vintages, the current wines of the house, for many of which, especially the red Hermitages, the Cornas and the Côte Rôtie, I

have a particular affection. Among the whites we tried were St-Péray, Chapoutier's Chante Alouette, Jaboulet's La Chapelle Hermitage 1950; for those who prefer, and can afford, old burgundies and bordeaux there is a well-stocked cellar of fine vintages.

Galantine de caneton: The name is misleading to English ears. It is a whole boned duck, its flesh mixed with finely minced pork, truffles, brandy and foie gras, sewn up in the skin of the duck and cooked in the oven; the result resembles a long fat sausage with the feet of the duck protruding at one end. This pâté has a flavour of very great delicacy, and is served sliced and quite unadorned. The lettuce leaves and the little heap of potato salad which, I have an uneasy feeling, would be the inevitable garnish provided by an English restaurateur, is simply unthinkable here.

Sole meunière: Perfectly cooked whole sole with quantities of hissing and foaming butter. Again, no garnish of any kind, and none needed.

Blettes à la crème au gratin: Blettes, or chard, that spinach-like vegetable with fleshy white stalks is, to me, only tolerable when cooked by a master hand, but as the Barattero chef has that hand, and makes a particularly excellent cream sauce, all was well.

After an exhausting day's driving in bad weather, and a good and not expensive lunch at the Cygne (but unsettling contemporary decor in an old hotel) in the rather depressing town of Le Puy, we returned to dinner at Lamastre.

Potage de légumes: The routine vegetable soup of the day, but the mixture of carrots, potatoes and other vegetables was so delicate, so buttery, so full of flavour, that this alone would serve to make the reputation of a lesser restaurant. Note: although so full of flavour this soup was quite thin. I think we make our vegetable soups too thick in this country.

Ris de veau à la crème: I have eaten too many ambitiously conceived but ill-executed dishes of sweetbreads ever again to order them of my own accord, so I was grateful to Madame Barattero for showing me how good they can be when properly done. There were mushrooms in the sauce. Perfect.

Petits pois à la française: A big bowl of very small fresh peas (even in good restaurants it is rare nowadays not to get *petits pois de conserve*) cooked with little shreds of lettuce but without the little onions usually associated with the *à la française* manner of cooking them. The result was very creamy and good. I doubt if I shall ever again put onions with my peas.

54

Pain d'écrevisses sauce cardinal: A very remarkable dish. A variety of *quenelle*, but unlike the pasty *quenelles* one eats elsewhere, even in the much cracked-up Lyon restaurants; as light as a puff of air, with the subtle and inimitable flavour of river crayfish permeating both *quenelle* and the rich cream sauce. The garnish of the dish consisted of a few whole scarlet crayfish and crescents of puff pastry.

Poularde en vessie: A 3-lb Bresse chicken, stuffed with its own liver, a little foie gras and slices of truffle, is tied up inside a pig's bladder and cooked extremely gently in a marmite of barely simmering water for one and a half hours. As Madame Barattero said, a chicken poached in the ordinary way, however carefully, cannot help but be '*un peu délavé*', a trifle washed out. By this system, which is an ancient one, the chicken, untouched by the cooking liquid, emerges with all its juices and flavours intact. When it is cold, as it was served to us, these juices formed inside the bladder have solidified to a small amount of clear and delicately flavoured jelly. Madame asserted that nothing was easier to cook than this dish – 'What do you mean, why can you not get a pig's bladder in England? You have pigs, do you not?' – and upheld her point by adding that the chef's eight-year-old son already knows how to prepare the *poulardes en vessie.* A green salad with cream in the dressing was the only accompaniment to the chicken.

The most important part of Friday's meal was a sad disappointment. It was a dish of tiny grilled lamb cutlets, obviously beautiful meat, but much too undercooked for our taste. On Saturday evening, when *épaule d'agneau* was announced, I explained the trouble. The little shoulder appeared cooked to what was, for us, perfection. A beautiful golden brown on the outside and just faintly pink in the middle. It had been preceded by a delicious *omelette aux champignons* and was accompanied by a *gratin* of courgettes and tomatoes, just slightly flavoured with garlic and cooked in butter instead of olive oil as it would have been in Provence. It went admirably with the lamb, and this was a good example of a very nice dinner of quite ordinary French dishes without any particular regional flavour or speciality of the house.

Next day was Whitsunday and we stayed in to lunch as
56 well as to dinner, for, as the weekend drew near, we had

been observing with fascinated interest the preparations afoot for the large number of customers expected for the *fêtes*. The chef had prepared fifteen of his boned and stuffed ducks and by lunchtime on Sunday dozens of *poulardes* tied up in pigs' bladders and scores of *pains d'écrevisses* were ready, all gently murmuring in their respective copper marmites.

Until now the service at meal times had been performed entirely by Marthe and Marie, the two pretty, expertly trained young girls in black frocks and starched white aprons who also brought our breakfasts and looked after our rooms. Now two waiters and Madame's sister from St-Vallier appeared upon the scene. There was no bustle and no panic or noise. Everything went like clockwork. And this I think partly explains what must seem a mystery to many visitors: how these unassuming places, in which the hotel part of the business is only incidental, can manage to maintain, day after day, cooking of a quality which simply could not be found in England and which is rare even in France. The answer is that they are organized and run in a way which a Guards sergeant-major would envy, and are as well equipped to deal with a banquet for three hundred people or a steady stream of holiday visitors as they are to provide comfort and an intimate atmosphere for a handful of regular guests out of season.

From a peaceful Sunday morning gossip in the charming blue and turquoise and cream tiled *charcuterie* run by

M. and Madame Montagne (where there is a good restaurant in a French town or village you may be sure that a good *charcuterie* is not far away), I returned to Barattero's for the promised Sunday feast. Customers were arriving from Valence, from Marseilles, from Lyon. A huge shining silver-grey Rolls-Bentley was parked in the square (it was the first English car we had seen). A party of young people flung themselves off their Lambrettas and clattered round a large table. They evidently took the cooking and its reputation for granted, for they hadn't dressed up or put on Sunday voices as we would have here for such an occasion. It was enjoyable to watch them, and all the other customers who were there simply because they were going to enjoy the food, for there was none of that holy hush which to some of us makes the grander eating places such a sore trial.

This was our luncheon menu.

Saucisse en feuilletage: This might be called the apotheosis of the sausage roll. A fresh, pure pork sausage (from the Montagne establishment, as I had already learned), coarsely cut and weighing about ¾ lb, is poached and then encased in flaky pastry, baked, and served hot, cut in slices. Both sausage and pastry were first-class. A delicious hors-d'œuvre.

Pain d'écrevisses sauce cardinal: This seemed even better, if possible, than the first time we had eaten it, and this is quite a test, for one is inclined to be more critical when tasting a famous dish for the second time. The chef at Barattero's has been cooking the *pain d'écrevisses*, and the other specialities of the house, almost every day for some thirty years, but even so I suppose it is possible that they might vary.

Artichauts Escoffier: I am always in two minds about dishes of this kind. The cream sauce with mushrooms was very light and did not overwhelm the artichoke hearts, but all the same I wonder if they are not better quite plain; at La Mère Brazier's in Lyon we had had a salad of whole artichoke hearts and lettuce dressed simply with a little oil and lemon, which, in its extreme simplicity, was quite delicious and the best artichoke dish I have ever eaten.

Poulet rôti: A *poulet de grain* (the equivalent of a spring chicken) for two people, perfectly roasted in butter, already carved but reconstituted into its original shape, served on a long platter with a nest of miniature *pommes rissolées* beside it. No other garnish.

For dinner that evening we tasted again the wonderful duck pâté, to be followed by a little roast *gigot* and another dish of those tender little *petits pois.* When we told the waiter how much we had enjoyed the lamb, he replied yes, certainly, it must be a treat to us after the mutton boiled with mint of English cookery. Some very quaint notions of English food are current in France.

The last customers were only just leaving as we ourselves said goodbye to Madame Barattero after dinner, for 59 we were leaving early next morning. The place had seemed full to us, but it was the time of the Algerian crisis, and had it not been for *les évènements*, Madame said, there would have been twice as many people. Customers would have come even from Paris. In her long, arduous and successful career as restaurateur and hotel keeper she had learned that you can never be quite sure what to expect, and even with her tremendous experience it is impossible to know how many people to cater for. As she says: 'Thirty-four years in the hotel business, what a stint, *hein*?'

Vogue, September 1958

Since writing my introductory note to the above I have received reassuring news of the food at the Hôtel du Midi. In June 1983 a reader who had stayed at Lamastre as a result of reading about Madame Barattero in *French Provincial Cooking* wrote me a charming letter telling me that the dinner had been 'most delicious'. The first course had been a *salade tiède* – '*ce que nous avons ici de la nouvelle cuisine*', she was told – but as you would expect subtle and different, followed by the celebrated *pain d'écrevisses* (the crayfish now come from Hungary), then there were cheeses, and a *chariot de desserts*, stylish, original '*d'un goût très raffiné*'. '*Tout est léger ici*', said the maître d'hôtel. There was an iced *soufflé aux marrons*, a pistachio sorbet, oranges in grenadine, *tuile tulips* filled with a cream of strawberries served with a *coulis*. Bernard, son of maître Perrier, the chef who became Madame Barattero's partner, and inherited from her the restaurant and hotel, of which he is now in charge, has succeeded his father as chef. It was Bernard, I learned, who had added the delicious desserts. The maître d'hôtel had said that they were the only missing elements in the range of dishes in the old days, and they are Bernard's contribution. I remember Bernard Perrier as a small boy, and I remember also how Madame Barattero predicted that in time he would follow in his father's footsteps. It was good to hear that the young man is fulfilling Madame's prophecy and that the Hôtel du Midi continues to flourish.

Measurements and Temperatures

from *Spices, Salts and Aromatics in the English Kitchen*

How much cheese is a handful? How much more or less is a cupful? What is the capacity of a glass, a tumbler, or soup ladle? What is the difference between a suspicion and a pinch? How much more is a good pinch? How much wine is a little, how many olives a few? When the book says a tin of chopped almonds or pomegranate juice what are you supposed to understand by that?

The answer to that one, at least, I know. A tin is an English round fifty-cigarette tin, at one time a fairly common unit of measurement in Egypt and other parts of North Africa and the Middle East. It holds 8 fl oz, the same as an American measuring cup. When I see this unit occurring in a traveller's cookery book I feel reassured that the recipe is genuine, probably written down from dictation by some Berber, Persian or Sudanese cook. Infuriating instructions, though, to anyone not in the know. In the same way, some of the best of old French recipes are the kind which specify '*un bol de crème fraîche*' or '*un verre de farine*'. Maddening until one twigs that the French have a different word for every kind of bowl they use, and a '*bol*' is not a salad bowl or a mixing bowl of unspecified capacity, but the bowl from which you drink your morning café au lait, in fact a cup: so to use it as a measuring unit is perfectly reasonable since every French household possesses – or did possess – such bowls, and their capacities, $\frac{1}{2}$ pint near enough, vary little.

Those glasses of flour, it can usually be taken, are tumblers of 6-oz capacity, because if French cooks mean a wine glass they say '*un verre à Bordeaux*' and if they mean a small wine glass they say '*un verre à porto*' – a sherry glass to us.

English teacups, breakfast cups and coffee cups used as measuring units make sense to us; there could hardly not be a teacup in the house; give or take a spoonful its capacity is always about 5 oz; a breakfast cup is 7 to 8 oz; a coffee cup is an after-dinner coffee cup, or $2\frac{1}{2}$ oz; but not to Americans, who are baffled by these terms in English cookery books. To them a cup is a measuring cup of 8 fl. oz capacity and there the matter ends. They don't know what a teacup holds, nor what a breakfast cup looks like, and a coffee cup is a morning coffee cup, which might be a teacup or a breakfast cup, whereas an after-dinner coffee cup is a demi-tasse.

As for scales and weights, in American household cooking they scarcely exist. The American system of measuring liquids and dry solids in standard cups and tablespoons is not very accurate but eliminates clutter in the way of measuring apparatus and means that everyone knows where they are when they read American recipes. Except, 63 that is to say, ourselves. Because when we are told that the American measuring cup contains exactly a half pint of liquid we are often not told also that the American pint is 16 oz whereas our Imperial pint is 20 oz. Although it wasn't, until 1878; a point which one has to remember when attempting to adapt recipes from eighteenth- and the earlier nineteenth-century books. Subtract 8 oz from each of those quarts of stock and wine, milk and cream specified in the older books and it makes quite a difference. Anyone, therefore, who uses American cookery books and American translations of foreign cookery books published in England, without clear indications as to the system of measurement used, needs to remember that the American pint is the pre-1878 English one of 16 oz, and that a quart in American terms means 32 oz.

Where I find the American measurement system messy, unreliable and time-wasting is when it comes to cramming sticky things like butter or fat into a cup – incidentally, a stick of butter, sometimes specified in American recipes, means 4 oz, a unit in which you can buy butter in the States – and I have never been very successful in measuring cooked ingredients such as chopped meat or diced potatoes in cups. Do you cram the stuff down? Do you give it a good rattle so that it settles – or alternatively flies all over the place? Just press lightly, my American colleagues tell me. How light is lightly? And how much does

it matter?

Recipes in which every last drop of lemon juice and grain of pepper are specified are often no more logical than the ones which throw out instructions to 'chop a handful of shallots' or 'braise a nice piece of beef'. If you are going to be told exactly how much of everything to use, at precisely what stage each ingredient is to be added, plus cooking temperatures and timing down to the final minute, then you require to be told also the weight and dimensions of the cooking pot you are to use and the material of which it is to be made; variations for every type of fuel would have to be allowed for, not to mention qualifications such as the temperature of your kitchen and the altitude at which you are cooking; after all you might want to know how long it takes to boil an egg when you reach the top of Mont Blanc.

There is surely a happy medium. It is quite possible to combine the exercise of one's five senses in the kitchen with the use of measuring devices as guides. By temperament a non-measurer, I have myself, first through the wish to communicate recipes and now by force of habit, become the reverse. I find that the discipline of weighing and measuring does one's cooking nothing but good, provided that one does not waste time messing about with quarter-saltspoons and five-eighths of pints, nor, above all, expect that precision will eliminate the necessity to keep one's head or train one's eye and palate.

Les Potages: Soups

from *French Provincial Cooking*

The making of a good soup is quite an art, and many otherwise clever cooks do not possess the *tour de main* necessary to its successful preparation. Either they over-complicate the composition of the dish, or they attach only minor importance to it, reserving their talents for the meal itself, and so it frequently happens that the soup does not correspond in quality to the rest of the dishes; nevertheless, the quality of the soup should foretell that of the entire meal.

Madame Seignobos, who wrote those words some fifty years ago in a book called *Comment on Forme une Cuisinière*, was probably referring to trained cooks, and does not mention those other happy-go-lucky ones who tell you, not without pride, 'Of course, I never follow a recipe, I just improvise as I go along. A little bit of this, a spoonful of that . . . it's much more fun, really.' Well, it may be more fun for the cook, but is seldom so diverting for the people who have to eat his products, because those people who have a sure enough touch to invent successfully in the kitchen without years of experience behind them are very rare indeed. The fortunate ones gifted with that touch are those who will also probably have the restraint to leave well alone when they *have* hit on something good;

66

the ones who can't resist a different little piece of embroidery every time they cook a dish will end by inducing a mood of gloomy apprehension in their families and guests. The domain of soup-making is one which comes in for more than its fair share of attention from the 'creative' cook, a saucepan of innocent-looking soup being a natural magnet to the inventive, and to those who pride themselves on their gifts for inspired improvisation.

I remember when I was very young being advised by the gastronomic authority among my contemporaries to take pretty well everything in the larder, including the remains of the salad (if I remember rightly some left-over soused herring was also included), tip it into a pan, add some water, and in due course, he said, some soup would emerge. I very soon learnt, from the results obtained by this method, that the soup-pot cannot be treated as though it were a dustbin. That lesson was elementary enough. The ones that are harder to assimilate are, first, in regard to the wisdom or otherwise of mixing too many ingredients, however good, to make one soup; the likelihood is that they will cancel each other out, so that although your soup may be a concentrated essence of good and nourishing ingredients it will not taste of anything in particular. Secondly, one has to learn in the end that the creative urge in the matter of embellishments is best kept under control. If your soup is already very good of its kind, possessed of its own true taste, will it not perhaps be spoilt by the addition of a few chopped olives, of a little piece of diced sausage, of a spoonful of paprika pepper? These are matters which everyone must decide for himself.

I know that many people think that their guests will find a simple vegetable soup dull, and so attempt to dress it up in some 'original' way. I don't think myself that a well-made vegetable soup, tasting fresh and buttery, and properly seasoned, is ever dull (I am talking about home-made soups).

In her beautiful book about Mexico *The Sudden View*, Sybille Bedford mentions 'a cream of vegetable soup which would have done honour to a household in the French Provinces before the war of 1870'. The phrase reminded me of the lovely soups made by Léontine, the cook of whose food I have already written in the pages about Paris household cookery in the introductory chapters to this book. These soups were anything but dull. They certainly were not complicated or expensive either: they belonged neither to *haute cuisine* nor to robust peasant cooking. They were, as befitted the household of a middle-class Norman family, in the direct line of French bourgeois and provincial cookery. Of course I did not know this at the time and did not think about it, I just enjoyed Léontine's delicious vegetable purées without the faintest idea why they were so good, but looking back now I remember how delicate and fresh they were, and I think they must have been the kind of soups Sybille Bedford had in mind when she wrote those lines.

Again, I remember the ordinary everyday soup of a provincial restaurant which has been famous for thirty years for its half-dozen rather grand specialities. These were, and are, beautiful dishes cooked and served to perfection, but the vegetable soups, made for the staff as well as for the customers, had just as much finesse in a different way. Composed of cheap vegetables such as carrots, potatoes and leeks, enriched with good butter and cream and faintly flavoured with parsley or chervil, made into purées of about the consistency of thin cream (I think we often make our cream soups too thick, too porridgy, in England, although I have heard people complain that French soups are too thin), they were soups which embodied so much of the charm, the flavours and scents of a country house kitchen garden that every evening while I stayed in that little hotel it was a struggle not to accept second or even third helpings of soup and so risk having no appetite left for the dishes to follow.

This is one of the dangers of a good soup. No doubt because the tin and the package have become so universal, people are astonished by the true flavours of a well-balanced home-made soup and demand more helpings if only to make sure that their noses and palates are not deceiving them. So it is always best to announce, as soon as the soup is served, what dishes are to follow, and not to go in for any false modesty in this respect. 'But there's nothing, absolutely nothing else coming' means, to the initiated, that there are going to be five courses of rather filling food. But it is kinder to guests to say so in a rather more direct manner.

The soup recipes in this book are mainly of the simple variety I have described. They are, on the whole, the kind most suitable to conditions in England. The ingredients are easily found; they are neither complicated nor costly. For those which require stock, I have described in detail how the best kind of meat broth, that from the *pot-au-feu*, is made. Not that one has to go through this performance every time one wants a little stock; but I do think it is essential that the principle should be understood. Once anybody has got the idea of a properly made broth into their heads, it is unlikely they will ever again resort to the hit and miss methods of the 'bundle it all into the stock-pot' school.

As far as the peasant and farmhouse soups, the *garbures* and the *potées* of traditional regional cookery go, I have only included one or two of these. In their way they are admirable, but heavy mixtures of pork and cabbage, beans and sausages and bread, constitute almost a whole meal in themselves, to be enjoyed by people who work hard all day in the open air; and I hope readers will excuse me for referring them to another volume, *French Country Cooking*, for recipes for this type of soup.

One more point. Although it is not necessary to know a great number of soups, it is highly desirable to have at least one well-tried recipe for every season of the year, and then one will not be led into the expense of buying out of season vegetables or into the error of unnecessary substitution. For example, the potato and tomato soup below, which is one of my favourites, also demands leeks. On several occasions I have tried, when leeks were out of season, using onions instead. Those who had not already eaten it cooked with leeks were probably unaware that anything was wrong, but I was myself quite conscious of the fact that the soup was not absolutely as it should have been. So I have given up trying to make the soup in the summer when no leeks are to be had; and serve instead a cream of fresh green peas, or the delicious *potage Crécy*, or the very light tomato soup described on page 74. If one is going to the trouble of preparing home-made soups one might as well have each one as good as possible of its kind.

POTAGE CRÈME DE TOMATES ET DE POMMES DE TERRE

Cream of Tomato and Potato Soup

The white part of 2 leeks, $\frac{1}{2}$ lb tomatoes, $\frac{3}{4}$ lb of potatoes, $1\frac{1}{2}$ oz butter, a little cream, chervil or parsley.

Melt the butter in a heavy saucepan; before it has bubbled put in the finely sliced leeks; let them just soften in the butter. Half the success of the soup depends upon this first operation. If the butter burns or the leeks brown instead of just melting the flavour will be spoilt.

Add the roughly chopped tomatoes; again let them cook until they start to give out their juice. Add the peeled and diced potato, a seasoning of salt and two lumps of sugar. Cover with 1¼ pints of water. After the soup comes to the boil let it simmer steadily but not too fast for 25 minutes. Put it through the food mill, twice if necessary. Return the purée to the rinsed-out saucepan. When it is hot, add about 4 oz of cream. In warm weather it is advisable to first bring this to the boil, as if it is not quite fresh it is liable to curdle when it makes contact with the acid of the tomatoes. Immediately before serving stir in a little chervil or very finely chopped parsley. Enough for four good helpings.

For all its simplicity and cheapness this is a lovely soup, in which you taste butter, cream and each vegetable, and personally I think it would be a mistake to add anything to it in the way of individual fantasies. It should not, however, be thicker than thin cream, and if it has come out too solid the addition of a little milk or water will do no harm.

The chef's soup known as *potage Solférino* is based on this purée of tomatoes, leeks and potatoes but is complicated, needlessly to my mind, with a final addition of little pieces of french beans and tiny marbles of potatoes scooped from large ones with a special implement.

POTAGE CRÉCY

Carrot Soup

¾ lb carrots, 1 large potato, 1 shallot or half a small onion, 1 oz butter, 1 pint veal, chicken or vegetable stock, or water if no stock is available, seasoning, parsley and chervil if possible.

Scrape the carrots, shred them on a coarse grater, put them together with the chopped shallot and the peeled and diced potato in a thick pan with the melted butter. Season with salt, pepper, a scrap of sugar. Cover the pan, and leave over a very low flame for about 15 minutes, until the carrots have almost melted to a purée. Pour over the stock, and simmer another 15 minutes. Sieve, return the purée to the pan, see that the seasoning is correct, add a little chopped parsley and some leaves of chervil. Enough for three.

Sometimes boiled rice is served separately with Crécy soup, which makes it pretty substantial. Fried bread-crumbs or small dice of fried potatoes are alternatives.

POTAGE BONNE FEMME

This old-fashioned French soup is the cheapest and one of the nicest of all vegetable soups.

1 lb potatoes, 3 carrots, 2 large leeks, 1½ oz butter, 2 pints water, seasoning. To finish the soup, a little cream, parsley, or chervil when available.

Melt the butter in your soup pan, put in the cleaned and finely sliced leeks and the diced carrots. Let them get thoroughly hot and saturated with the butter; add the peeled and diced potatoes, the water, a little salt, a lump or two of sugar. Cook steadily but not at a gallop for 25 to 30 minutes. Sieve through the finest mesh of the *mouli*, twice if necessary. Taste for seasoning, and when ready to serve add the cream, and parsley or chervil chopped very, very finely. Enough for four.

The carrots are not essential to the soup, but they add a little extra flavour and colour.

POTAGE DE TOMATES ESTIVAL

Light Tomato Soup

Slice 2 lb of ripe juicy tomatoes into a saucepan; add half an onion finely sliced and 2 teaspoons of salt. Cook with the lid on the pan, but without any liquid or butter, for 10 to 15 minutes, until the tomatoes are quite soft. Put through the food mill. In a bowl dilute 1 tablespoon of ground rice with a little cold milk. Stir this into the purée. Heat gently, and gradually add about 1½ pints of hot milk, or half milk and half light chicken or veal broth. Cook very gently, stirring often, for about 15 minutes until all traces of the little white globules formed by the ground rice have disappeared. It should be quite smooth, but if it is not, press it once more through a fine sieve. Stir in some very finely chopped parsley or chervil. Properly made, this very simple soup is most refreshing and delicate, but it can, if you prefer, be enriched with a little cream or a lump of butter stirred in before it is served, though it should remain on the thin side. Makes four to six helpings.

Cassoulet Toulousain

from *A Book of Mediterranean Food*

Of all the great dishes which French regional cookery has produced the cassoulet is perhaps the most typical of true country food, the genuine, abundant, earthy, richly flavoured and patiently simmered dish of the ideal farmhouse kitchen. Hidden beneath a layer of creamy, golden-crusted haricot beans in a deep, wide, earthen pot, the cassoulet contains garlicky pork sausages, smoked bacon, salt pork, a wing or leg of preserved goose, perhaps a piece of mutton, or a couple of pig's feet, or half a duck, and some chunks of pork rind. The beans are tender, juicy, moist but not mushy, aromatic smells of garlic and herbs escape from the pot as the cassoulet is brought smoking hot from the oven to the table. French novelists, gourmets, and cooks have devoted pages to praise of the cassoulet, and its fame spread from south-western France, where it originated, first to Paris restaurants, then all over France; recently it has achieved some popularity in this country, no doubt because it seems an attractive solution to the entertaining of a fairly large number of people with little fuss or expense.

A genuine cassoulet is not, however, a cheap dish. Neither are the materials always easy to find. When you consider that in the rich agricultural country of the Languedoc every farmer's wife has the ingredients of the dish within arm's length, festoons of sausages and hams hanging in her kitchen, jars of goose and pork preserved in their own fat on her larder shelves, you understand how the cassoulet came into being; it was evolved to make the best use of the local materials; when you have to go out and buy these things the cost is high (this is just as much the case in France as in England) and although quite a good dish can be made at moderate cost it should be remembered that tinned beans and sausages served in an earthenware casserole do not, alas, constitute a cassoulet.

Bear in mind, also, that a cassoulet is heavy and filling food, and should be kept for cold winter days, preferably for luncheons when none of the party has anything very active to do afterwards.

The ingredients for say 6 people are 1½ lb of good quality medium-sized white haricot beans (butter beans will not do, they are too floury), 1 lb of belly of pork, 1 lb of breast of mutton, ¼ lb of fresh rind of pork, or failing that of ham or bacon, 1 lb of fresh, coarse garlic sausage (not salame, but the kind sold for frying or boiling by French and Continental delicatessen shops), 2 or 3 pieces of preserved goose (in England replace this with half a duck, or omit it altogether), 1 lb of a cheap cut of smoked gammon, 2 or 3 cloves of garlic, herbs, 3 oz of goose dripping or pig's lard, an onion.

Soak the beans overnight. Put them in a large casserole or saucepan, add the onion, garlic, pork rind, the piece of gammon, and a faggot of herbs (bay leaf, thyme, parsley). Cover with fresh water and cook either in a slow oven for 4 to 5 hours or over a direct flame on top of the stove for $1\frac{1}{2}$ to 3 hours (the time of cooking varies a good deal with the quality of the beans). Add the salt only in the final stages of cooking.

Meanwhile, roast the pork and the mutton in the dripping (and the duck if you are using this).

When the beans are all but cooked, cut all the meats, the rinds and the sausage into convenient pieces, put them in alternate layers with the beans in a deep earthenware pot and add enough of the liquid in which the beans have cooked to come about half-way up. Put into a fairly slow oven (Regulo 3–4) uncovered, to finish cooking. This final operation can be prolonged to suit yourself by turning the oven right down. Eventually a brown crust forms on top of the beans. Stir this gently into the whole mass, and leave for another crust to form. Again stir it in, and when a third crust has formed the cassoulet should be ready. Sometimes the top is sprinkled with a layer of breadcrumbs when the pot is put in the oven and this speeds up the crusting of the cassoulet, and if perhaps you have added too much liquid the breadcrumbs should help to absorb it. Serve on very hot plates, with plenty of young red wine, and perhaps a green salad and a good cheese to finish the meal.

'I'll be with You in the Squeezing of a Lemon'

Oliver Goldsmith

from *An Omelette and a Glass of Wine*

In 1533 the Company of Leathersellers offered Henry the Eighth and Anne Boleyn a great banquet to celebrate Anne's coronation on Whit Sunday in Westminster Hall. Among the princely luxuries which graced the feast was one lemon, one only, for which the Leathersellers had paid six silver pennies.

Now that in England we pay an average of six copper pence per lemon, I think I would still find them almost worth the silver pennies which in 1533 must have represented a pretty large sum.

It is hard to envisage any cooking without lemons, and indeed those of us who remember the shortage or total absence of lemons during the war years, recall the lack as one of the very worst of the minor deprivations of those days.

Without a lemon to squeeze on to fried or grilled fish, no lemon juice to sharpen the flatness of the dried pulses – the red lentils, the split peas – which in those days loomed so largely in our daily diet, no lemon juice to help out the stringy ewe-mutton and the ancient boiling fowls of the time, no lemon juice for pancakes, no peel to grate into cake mixtures and puddings, we felt frustrated every 79 time we opened a cookery book or picked up a mixing bowl. In short, during the past four hundred years the lemon has become, in cooking, the condiment which has largely replaced the vinegar, the verjuice (preserved juice of green grapes), the pomegranate juice, the bitter orange juice, the mustard and wine compounds which were the acidifiers poured so freely into the cooking pots of sixteenth- and seventeenth-century Europe. There are indeed times when a lemon as a seasoning seems second only in importance to salt.

To Mediterranean cooking the juice of the lemon is vital. It is the astringent corrective, as well as the flavouring, for olive-oil-based dishes and fat meat. By English cooks this point is not and has never been sufficiently appreciated. For example a home-made brawn or pig's-head cheese seasoned with a generous amount of lemon juice (squeezed in after cooking and when the meat is shredded or chopped ready for potting or moulding) transforms an often insipid dish into a delicacy. And to me a lentil soup or purée is unthinkable without the complement of lemon and olive oil; then, just try to imagine lamb kebabs without lemon . . .

In scores of English and French creams, ices, cakes, soufflés, sweet omelettes and preserves, it is the aromatic oil contained in the peel or zest, rather than the juice, which is the operative part of the lemon. For these dishes choose thick-skinned fruit.

One of the best of lemon graters is lump sugar, although Hannah Glasse (*The Art of Cookery Made Plain and Easy*, 1747) who was perhaps partial to a pun, directed her readers to grate lemon skins with a piece of broken glass. Possibly in her day that practical little utensil known as a lemon zester had not yet been invented. And the lump sugar business, called for in so many recipes, is often exasperating because it is unexplained. When, however, it is remembered that sugar was bought in loaves, the whole procedure becomes logical. You simply hacked off a size-able lump, and with this big piece, rasped off the skin of the lemon, thus releasing the essential oil of the zest which is so important to the flavour of creams, ices, and particu-larly of that uniquely English speciality, lemon curd. This lovely dish does, of course, also include the juice of the lemons. So do all the lemon recipes which I have chosen for this article. There is something especially satisfactory about using the whole of the fruit in one dish. Even more satisfactory are the beautiful flavours and scents of these dishes authentically made and eaten when fresh. (Lemon curd has been one of the most painfully travestied and ill-used of all our true English preserves. No commercially made version gives so much as a hint of its true nature.)

To make 1 lb approximately, ingredients are: 2 large lemons, preferably thick-skinned; $\frac{1}{2}$ lb loaf sugar; 4 whole large eggs; $\frac{1}{4}$ lb of unsalted or slightly salted butter.

Rub sugar lumps on to the peel of the lemons, holding them over a bowl, until each lump starts crumbling, then start on another. About four lumps will rub sufficient outside peel and oil out of each lemon. Put all the sugar together into the bowl.

Squeeze the lemons, and strain the juice. Whisk the eggs very thoroughly with the strained juice.

Cut the butter into small cubes.

Set the bowl in, or over, a pan of water. When the sugar has dissolved add the eggs, then the butter. Stir until all ingredients are amalgamated and the whole mixture looks rather like thick honey, with about the same consistency. Remove the bowl (older cooks still find an old-fashioned stoneware jam jar the best vessel for making lemon curd. I prefer an open bowl. I like to see what's happening) and stir until the curd has cooled. Turn into small jars and cover with good quality kitchen parchment.

To the straightforward lemon curd, a couple of sponge fingers, broken up, are sometimes added. They thicken the curd, giving it extra body and making it more stable when spread into flan cases or flat, open plate pies. A richer alternative is a small proportion of ground almonds. Allow up to 2 oz for the quantities given.

Writers of old recipes often claimed that lemon curd keeps for years. Perhaps it does. I would say that three months is about the maximum, and that long before this period is up the confection, like a fresh fruit sorbet stored in the deep freeze, has lost its exquisite flavour and the edge has gone from the sharp scent.

Use lemon curd to make a delicious filling for little brown bread sandwiches to eat with ices, to spread on brioche or currant bread, or as a sauce for little yeast pancakes as well as for the traditional lemon curd pie made with rich, sweet short crust.

LEMON ICE CREAM

from *Summer Cooking*

2 lemons, 3 oz white sugar, $\frac{1}{4}$ pint double cream

Put the thinly peeled rind of the lemons with the white sugar in 4 oz of water, and simmer gently for 20 minutes. Leave the syrup to cool, strain and add to it the juice of the lemons. When quite cold, add it gradually to the whipped cream, stirring gently until the whole mixture is smooth. Freeze.

LEMON SOUFFLÉ

from *French Country Cooking*

4 eggs, 3 tablespoons castor sugar, the juice and rind of one lemon

Beat the yolks of the eggs with the sugar, the grated rind of the lemon and the juice, for several minutes. Whip the whites and fold them in. Pour into a buttered soufflé dish and cook for 10–12 minutes in a medium-hot oven.

Soufflés made without the addition of flour are very light and creamy, but the whole operation should be performed with speed.

The timing of soufflés is entirely a matter of experience and depends upon practice and the knowledge of one's own oven, so that while Regulo No. 7 is the set temperature for soufflés on my own gas cooker, the pressure varies considerably in different districts and according to the age of the stove. So before venturing upon a soufflé for a dinner party, it is wise to carry out a few experiments, noting the time taken and the temperature of the oven for the most successful.

Cottage Loaves

from *English Bread and Yeast Cookery*

Cottage loaves, as all professional bakers writing for their colleagues readily admit, are notoriously difficult to mould and bake, although I think that the main cause of my own difficulties with the making and baking of an English cottage loaf is the very particular and vivid memory I have of the cottage loaves of my childhood. It is the bread I remember best from those days, and it was the one we used for toasting in front of the coal fire in the nursery and later in the schoolroom. The loaves were large ones, and the topknots rather small, so the slices were irregular, and difficult to hold on the fork. The crumb was creamy and soft, the crust was always a bit scorched on one side, although it wasn't hard or tough. As I remember it, the topknot always leant to one side, in the way associated also with a brioche.

Our bread came from the village bakery, and I have since learned that the county of Sussex, where I grew up, was a region with a reputation for good, sweet-eating bread. This was probably because so many of the villages, in East Sussex particularly, were quite unspoiled, the shops retained their country character, the bakeries their old-fashioned ovens. It had been a region of many windmills 85 and watermills too, so there was a tradition of bread flour milled from good locally grown wheat.

The loaf I remember, baked on the floor of a brick-built, side-flue oven, would be impossible to reproduce in a modern domestic gas or electric one. The nearest to be got to it, for anyone who feels like going to the trouble, is to use the following notes concerning the dough for a cottage loaf, its proving and moulding, and the assembling of the two separate pieces, which is the crucial point.

1. The dough should be a fairly stiff one – but not too stiff, or the loaf will be hard.

2. The dough must be well-risen but not over-proved, or it will collapse.

3. After the first rising and the breaking down of the dough, it should be divided into two pieces, the one for the topknot weighing approximately one-third, or a little more, of the total; to get the proportions right the first time it will be necessary, therefore, first to weigh the whole piece of dough, then to divide it and weigh both pieces to check that they are approximately accurate. After two or three attempts the weighing can be eliminated, but at first it is difficult to judge simply by sight and feel.

4. For the second rising or proving, the two pieces should be kept separate. Roll each one into a ball, turning the folds of the bottom piece under, those of the topknot *upwards*. Cover both pieces, so that no skin forms on the dough.

5. Before the second proving is complete, i.e. after about 45

minutes instead of the more usual hour, the assembling of the two loaves is done in the following manner: slightly flatten the top of the bottom loaf, make a small cross-shaped cut, as for a Coburg, approximately $1\frac{1}{2}$ inches across. Now flatten, slightly, the base of the topknot and perch it on the bottom loaf. The flattening of the two pieces of dough is the absolutely key point of the assemblage of a cottage loaf. Without knowledge of this small detail – the only publication in which I have ever seen it given is the late Walter Banfield's splendid book *Manna* (1937) – it is almost impossible to make a successful cottage loaf. Without a flat surface on which to rest the topknot, the bottom piece of the loaf simply collapses under the superimposed weight, so the two loaves re-merge into one.

6. With your thumb and first two fingers joined to make a cone shape, press a hole through the centre of the topknot down into the main body of the loaf. This operation (the bakers call it bashing) effectively joins the two pieces and also gives the entirely characteristic appearance to the loaf.

7. The joining of the two loaves is a danger point. If it is performed with too violent a hand, it causes a serious disruption in the dough, and may distort the shape completely.

8. The assembled cottage loaf should now be covered, preferably with an inverted pot or deep bowl, and left to recover after its handling, but not for too long, or it will spread and lose its shape before you get it into the oven. Ten minutes should be ample time for this final ripening but, if the dough is at all

too slack and looks in the least bit like collapsing, put it straight into the oven. Do not, in any case, preheat the oven. Turn it to 450°F, 230°C, gas no. 8 or 9, immediately before putting in the loaf, on the lower shelf. As the oven heats up, so the loaf expands. I learned this method through talking to Louie Mayer about Virginia Woolf and her bread-baking. Mrs Mayer told me that for many years the cooking at the Woolfs' house at Rodmell was all done on an old Florence oil-fired cooker. The overhead plate rack was a good place to put the bread dough while it was rising. When ready to bake the shaped loaf was put straight into the cool oven. As the heat built up the loaf grew. Mrs Mayer was not aware that there was anything unusual about the method. When the oil cooker was replaced with an electric one, she went on baking her bread in the same way and it still worked. I too found that it worked quite well with my gas-fired oven, but with natural gas it is advisable to wait at least 5 minutes after lighting the oven, or the top crust of the loaf may get badly burned. In an electric oven the system works better, and can be applied to many other kinds of bread, always providing that the dough still has some spring left in it – in other words, as already explained, it must be slightly under-proved.

9. After 30 minutes, when the loaf has risen and taken shape, it is a good idea to cover it with a bowl – if you have one sufficiently deep – in order to prevent the crust becoming too hard and tough. But towards the end of baking time, uncover

the loaf again to let out the steam and for any final browning of the crust which may be necessary.

I cannot say that, even with all these efforts and tricks, the cottage loaf of beloved memory emerges, but at least a loaf of approximately the correct shape and with a good flavour and excellent moist crumb can be produced.

10. The flours and the proportions I use are as follows: $1\frac{1}{2}$ lb of strong plain unbleached flour, $\frac{1}{2}$ lb of an 81 per cent wheat-meal such as Prewett's Millstone or Jordan's Country Cook-book bread flour, just over $\frac{1}{2}$ oz of yeast, $\frac{3}{4}$ oz of salt, 1 pint or a little less of warm water. (US equivalents: $5\frac{1}{2}$ cups or so unbleached all-purpose flour and $\frac{1}{2}$ cup whole-wheat flour; good $\frac{1}{2}$ oz yeast ($1\frac{1}{4}$ tsp dry); 1 tsp salt; $2\frac{1}{2}$ cups water, or less.) Very great care must be taken not to make the dough too slack.

PENGUIN 60s

MARTIN AMIS · *God's Dice*
HANS CHRISTIAN ANDERSEN · *The Emperor's New Clothes*
MARCUS AURELIUS · *Meditations*
JAMES BALDWIN · *Sonny's Blues*
AMBROSE BIERCE · *An Occurrence at Owl Creek Bridge*
DIRK BOGARDE · *From Le Pigeonnier*
WILLIAM BOYD · *Killing Lizards*
POPPY Z. BRITE · *His Mouth will Taste of Wormwood*
ITALO CALVINO · *Ten Italian Folktales*
ALBERT CAMUS · *Summer*
TRUMAN CAPOTE · *First and Last*
RAYMOND CHANDLER · *Goldfish*
ANTON CHEKHOV · *The Black Monk*
ROALD DAHL · *Lamb to the Slaughter*
ELIZABETH DAVID · *I'll be with You in the Squeezing of a Lemon*
N. J. DAWOOD (TRANS.) · *The Seven Voyages of Sindbad the Sailor*
ISAK DINESEN · *The Dreaming Child*
SIR ARTHUR CONAN DOYLE · *The Man with the Twisted Lip*
DICK FRANCIS · *Racing Classics*
SIGMUND FREUD · *Five Lectures on Psycho-Analysis*
KAHLIL GIBRAN · *Prophet, Madman, Wanderer*
STEPHEN JAY GOULD · *Adam's Navel*
ALASDAIR GRAY · *Five Letters from an Eastern Empire*
GRAHAM GREENE · *Under the Garden*
JAMES HERRIOT · *Seven Yorkshire Tales*
PATRICIA HIGHSMITH · *Little Tales of Misogyny*
M. R. JAMES AND R. L. STEVENSON · *The Haunted Dolls' House*
RUDYARD KIPLING · *Baa Baa, Black Sheep*
PENELOPE LIVELY · *A Long Night at Abu Simbel*
KATHERINE MANSFIELD · *The Escape*

PENGUIN 60s

GABRIEL GARCÍA MÁRQUEZ · *Bon Voyage, Mr President*
PATRICK MCGRATH · *The Angel*
HERMAN MELVILLE · *Bartleby*
SPIKE MILLIGAN · *Gunner Milligan, 954024*
MICHEL DE MONTAIGNE · *Four Essays*
JAN MORRIS · *From the Four Corners*
JOHN MORTIMER · *Rumpole and the Younger Generation*
R. K. NARAYAN · *Tales from Malgudi*
ANAÏS NIN · *A Model*
FRANK O'CONNOR · *The Genius*
GEORGE ORWELL · *Pages from a Scullion's Diary*
CAMILLE PAGLIA · *Sex and Violence, or Nature and Art*
SARA PARETSKY · *A Taste of Life*
EDGAR ALLAN POE · *The Pit and the Pendulum*
MISS READ · *Village Christmas*
JEAN RHYS · *Let Them Call It Jazz*
DAMON RUNYON · *The Snatching of Bookie Bob*
SAKI · *The Secret Sin of Septimus Brope*
WILL SELF · *Scale*
GEORGES SIMENON · *Death of a Nobody*
MURIEL SPARK · *The Portobello Road*
ROBERT LOUIS STEVENSON · *The Pavilion on the Links*
PAUL THEROUX · *Down the Yangtze*
WILLIAM TREVOR · *Matilda's England*
MARK TULLY · *Ram Chander's Story*
JOHN UPDIKE · *Friends from Philadelphia*
EUDORA WELTY · *Why I Live at the P. O.*
EDITH WHARTON · *Madame de Treymes*
OSCAR WILDE · *The Happy Prince*
VIRGINIA WOOLF · *Killing the Angel in the House*

READ MORE IN PENGUIN

For complete information about books available from Penguin and how to order them, please write to us at the appropriate address below. Please note that for copyright reasons the selection of books varies from country to country.

IN THE UNITED KINGDOM: Please write to *Dept. JC, Penguin Books Ltd, FREEPOST, West Drayton, Middlesex UB7 0BR.*
If you have any difficulty in obtaining a title, please send your order with the correct money, plus ten per cent for postage and packaging, to *PO Box No. 11, West Drayton, Middlesex UB7 0BR.*

IN THE UNITED STATES: Please write to *Consumer Sales, Penguin USA, P.O. Box 999, Dept. 17109, Bergenfield, New Jersey 07621-0120.* VISA and MasterCard holders call 1-800-253-6476 to order all Penguin titles.

IN CANADA: Please write to *Penguin Books Canada Ltd, 10 Alcorn Avenue, Suite 300, Toronto, Ontario M4V 3B2.*

IN AUSTRALIA: Please write to *Penguin Books Australia Ltd, P.O. Box 257, Ringwood, Victoria 3134.*

IN NEW ZEALAND: Please write to *Penguin Books (NZ) Ltd, Private Bag 102902, North Shore Mail Centre, Auckland 10.*

IN INDIA: Please write to *Penguin Books India Pvt Ltd, 706 Eros Apartments, 56 Nehru Place, New Delhi 110 019.*

IN THE NETHERLANDS: Please write to *Penguin Books Netherlands bv, Postbus 3507, NL-1001 AH Amsterdam.*

IN GERMANY: Please write to *Penguin Books Deutschland GmbH, Metzlerstrasse 26, 60594 Frankfurt am Main.*

IN SPAIN: Please write to *Penguin Books S. A., Bravo Murillo 19, 1o B, 28015 Madrid.*

IN ITALY: Please write to *Penguin Italia s.r.l., Via Felice Casati 20, I-20124 Milano.*

IN FRANCE: Please write to *Penguin France S. A., 17 rue Lejeune, F-31000 Toulouse.*

IN JAPAN: Please write to *Penguin Books Japan, Ishikiribashi Building, 2-5-4, Suido, Bunkyo-ku, Tokyo 112.*

IN GREECE: Please write to *Penguin Hellas Ltd, Dimocritou 3, GR-106 71 Athens.*

IN SOUTH AFRICA: Please write to *Longman Penguin Southern Africa (Pty) Ltd, Private Bag X08, Bertsham 2013.*